Widow's Peak

A Common Woman's Most Uncommon Story
Jean Elizabeth Radcliffe
1924 – 2011

Liz McCarty
h. Alton Jones

Printed in the United States of America

ISBN: 978-0-9845545-1-5

Also by h. Alton Jones: *The Man on the Bench*
(*www.TheManOnTheBench.com*)

54 Candles Publishing
8369 N. Via Linda
Scottsdale, AZ 85258

www.54Candles.org

This book is dedicated to all the women of the world whose indomitable spirits have carried them through the most challenging and difficult times imaginable and in so doing have shouldered the burden of civilization since the beginnings of time.

A special thanks to **Hospice of the Valley**. The wonderful people on the staff go way beyond what we had thought possible to help maintain comfort and dignity during life's final passage. I don't know where we would have been without them.

Cover photos are from Detroit, Michigan mostly in the 1930s and 1940s. They include images of key places mentioned in this book including Federal's Department Store, Wonder Bread bakery and Cooley High School.

Introduction

It was warm and humid in Detroit, Michigan on July 25, 1924. On that day, Tella Jane Radcliffe, a transplant from Cleveland, Tennessee, gave birth to her third daughter, Jean "Elizabeth" Radcliffe.

The twenties were roaring. The auto industry was booming. Detroit's population swelled as jobs with Ford, General Motors, Hudson, Chrysler and the other auto companies were plentiful. Starting with nothing, William Clarence Radcliffe worked long and hard to provide for his family. About the time their fourth and final daughter, Evelyn Jane (Priscilla) Radcliffe was born, the stock market crashed and the country was plunged into the economic darkness of the Great Depression. The Radcliffe family went into survival mode. As the sun rose on a cold New Year's Day in 1930, Clarence and Tella Jane were faced with the daunting task of providing for ten year old Virginia, seven year old Marion, five year old Elizabeth and the infant Priscilla. Clarence was without a job. It was a darker morning than most.

What follows is the story of my mother, Elizabeth. It is written in her words, painstakingly elicited and transcribed by my wife, Liz McCarty. Over the previous quarter century, Liz and my mother had grown to know and love one another and in many respects depend upon each other for warmth and support when needed. When Liz decided to undertake this project, Elizabeth was pleased and excited. Liz proved to be the ideal catalyst to bring out her story. As co-members of the "female race", they could talk about things openly and in ways that only "the girls" can do. Even though Elizabeth knew her sons and family members would ultimately read her words, she said things she could never have said in my presence. And she often laughed about it. Sometimes, she would cry.

Although she was close to her two older sisters, Virginia and Marion, until they died, she spent most of her years in their shadows. Both were academically high achievers. Marion was a radiant beauty. Virginia was a spectacularly talented musician. I remember when I was a child living on Virginia's farm in Ohio, if an object could be made to vibrate, whether with air currents, a hammer, a string or anything else, Virginia could play it and play it beautifully. Both Marion and Virginia were so talented and gifted that even if a younger sibling had outstanding skills, she would be hard pressed to avoid some feelings of inferiority. And as the third child, Elizabeth didn't hold any particular "special place" in the eyes of her mother. Despite her love for her older sisters, Elizabeth spent most of her life trying to "catch up". That sad reality will come to play in many of the stories you're about to read.

The following auto-biography is structured in a slightly different fashion than you might expect. In the course of most of the interviews, there was a single, dominant line of questioning that might logically be construed as a "chapter". However, the chapters are broken down by the date of the interview. In some cases, the principal subject of discussion spans more than one interview. Here is the reasoning behind that decision.

I have been called to my mother's death bed three times in my life. In each case, the doctors believed there was no chance of survival. Once in 1974, her rear engine Volkswagen was struck head-on by a drunken motorcyclist traveling at 100 miles per hour. She miraculously pulled through, but that was in the days when blood wasn't being tested for the deadly disease hepatitis C. Although she unexpectedly survived the night, the transfusions required to keep her alive would be the beginning of the end. The disease was to lie undetected for nearly twenty-five years before it reared its ugly head and nearly put her down again.

The next call came just before Thanksgiving in 2006. The effects of the hepatitis gradually diminished her liver function and resulted in a poisoning of the brain. She lapsed into a coma and was taken to the Mayo Clinic Hospital. The medical team told me she would never

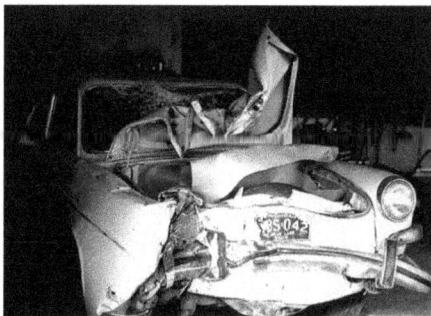
The car following Elizabeth's first encounter with death

come out of the coma. This tough-as-nails woman fought her way back to life. The story of that fight is an amazing account of the indomitability of the human spirit and the importance of music in life. I will include an account of that story in an appendix at the end of this book.

However, the point is this – Elizabeth experienced a nearly unparalleled amount of physical pain and suffering in her lifetime. Between the aforementioned, bouts with shingles, arthritis, shattered legs and various other unfortunate encounters with misfortune, Elizabeth spent the last years of her life in excruciating pain. Despite this, she retained her sense of humor and wit until the very end. But while living alone, she wasn't always a master of administration when it came to her pain medications. You will notice that during some interviews, she had greater clarity of mind and better mental focus than in some others. By defining the chapters according to the date of the interviews, we present contiguous blocks of information spoken with the same mindset and mental condition.

As I read through the preliminary transcriptions, there were a number of questions concerning the accuracy of some of the stories, particularly when it came to dates. In some cases, I have added parenthetical clarifications below Elizabeth's actual statements. Sometimes, clarity of mind fogged her memory. On other occasions, she simply saw things differently than other observers.

Prior to the death of her oldest sister, she would sometimes talk of her frustration resulting from her regular conversations with Virginia. It would anger her when she and her sister talked in depth about something that had occurred fifty or sixty years prior. "Virginia insists that it didn't happen the way I know it did", she would say. "She's still the older bully sister. And I know it happened this other way."

"Mom, your version is correct, even if it's wrong," I would tell her. "This is your story. It's about your perceptions, about the things you've seen and done. If it's your story, there is only one correct and true version and that's the one you tell. Virginia is welcome to tell her story and as such, it too is correct and true. But this story is yours."

I would tell her about cases in history where the most accepted versions of historical events came from the last person talking. For example, Wyatt Earp outlived all his brothers and the others that were present at the "Shoot-out at the OK Corral". Wyatt's story may not be 100% historically accurate, but it's the most compelling, the most recent and nobody was left alive to refute it. "Tell your story, Mom, not someone else's."

In the course of telling her story, Elizabeth sometimes mentions names with whom you may be unfamiliar. I've included a small "family tree" in an appendix for your reference.

The story you're about to read is about a woman growing up in the Great Depression, reaching adulthood as World War II was coming to a close, raising a family as the Great American Dream came to fruition and growing strong and independent as women in this nation asserted themselves to say they could achieve and reach the highest peak on the mountain of life. It provides insights into the condition of our nation from the roaring twenties through the first decade of the 21st century. There are little tidbits of history buried throughout the book. There are glimpses of how a repressed spirit ultimately breaks free and how that spirit has been at the vanguard of human progress throughout the millennia. It is the story of a most uncommon, common woman. It is the story of a lifetime.

h. Alton Jones
June 2013

On Mother's Day 2010, my husband and I gave his mother a book. It was created by Pamela and Stephen Pavuk and is intended as a guide for writing a life history. I thought it would be interesting to sit with my mother-in-law and ask her the questions in the book and record her stories. I wasn't sure she would be willing to do this, but the first day I arrived at her home to begin our session she was waiting eagerly. She had decided that I was going to make a book with these stories.

Throughout her life, she had managed to save some priceless keepsakes and as her stories began to unfold, she would remember that she had something. The next week when I came to hear her wonderful dialog, she would give me her treasured item and ask that I include it in "the book".

Her sense of humor was so evident that I can't help but laugh when I read this. Following are my interviews with a very special woman that I only thought I knew before I embarked on this project.

Widow's Peak
The Story of a Lifetime
A Keepsake of Personal Memoirs
Jean Elizabeth Radcliffe

Interviewed by Liz McCarty

June 22, 2010

If your ancestors migrated from another country, from where did they come?

It's too far back for me to know. I was told that my father's family came from England before the Revolutionary War. My mother's family came from England and Germany. My mother's family had land in downtown Berlin. They never went back to Germany to claim it. Some of each family settled in Georgia and Tennessee.

James & Maranda Ratcliff c 1890

What do you remember about the oldest relative you knew personally?

A pocket-watch left at the Ratcliff jewelry store nearly 100 years ago and it still keeps perfect time.

I remember my father's mother's twin sister. His father married her after his wife died. When my father came out of the service, his name was spelled Radcliffe instead of Ratcliff. He did not want to go to the trouble of changing it so he just started spelling it that way.

I met my father's aunt. She was in her nineties and still had no gray hair. Virginia asked her what she did to keep the color in her hair and she said she rinsed it with tea.

My father's father owned the only jewelry store in Cleveland, Tennessee.

When and where were your mother's mother and father born?

Both were born in Cleveland, Tennessee.

What was her mother's maiden name? Fullbright

Describe them. What kind of people were they?

We went to Cleveland, Tennessee every summer from Michigan until I graduated from grade school. My grandfather was delightful. When he visited Michigan he came by himself. He loved to go shopping and liked to spend his time in the shoe department. He described it as being more fun than the circus.

When your grandfather came from Tennessee to visit you, how did he get there?

He must have taken the train. It could have been the bus, but I'm not sure. It very likely was the bus because the bus stopped in Cleveland and I don't remember ever seeing the train stop there.

My grandmother tried to be warm and would hug us. But we never liked to touch her because her skin was so soft. She was on the heavy side and developed sugar diabetes. I think that might have been what killed her. She only came to Michigan once when my mother was very ill. My mother had a nervous

Gerome Lee & Ada Goodner early 1950s

breakdown. She was about 40. I remember Marion walking my

mother down the stairs and my mother did not recognize her mother. Marion had to tell her who she was and then she remembered.

Grandmother was a marvelous cook and made the best biscuits in the world. They always had ham. They had a farm that belonged to my grandmother's father. A lot of their food supply came from the farm. They lived in the city in a home with five bedrooms. Sometimes we went for Thanksgiving in Tennessee. We always had turkey when we were there for Thanksgiving.

The one thing I had a hard time forgiving Mother for was a gramophone. It had a wax cylinder and was beautifully decorated. My father had recorded a song on the wax cylinder. It was the song he sang at his mother's bedside as she was dying. He had a beautiful tenor voice. She never asked any of the daughters if they wanted it and she gave the gramophone to Willard. Willard said he never got it. Just a few nights ago I dreamed about this. Priscilla had been asked to ship it. I now wonder if she sold it instead.

June 29, 2010

If you have inherited any characteristics of your mother's parents, describe what they are and how you feel about them.

I met my mother's parents. I really didn't spend much time there. I spent most of the time at Margaret and Mac's house. That's my mother's younger sister. From what I understand Grandmother Goodner was a strong-willed person and so according to Howard I have inherited that through my mother. But that's the only thing I can think of.

How do you feel about that?

How do I feel about it? Well, it has its good points and its bad points. It [laughs] well, it doesn't bother me. She was a good woman. She was strong-willed, but some women have to be strong-willed and my grandfather was probably easily led, I guess you might say.

She would do beautiful quilting work and did all of the sewing. When the children were young she made all of their clothes. Most families did that back then. My mother was a very good seamstress, very good. And so I guess I learned by questioning her about things. So I guess I got the sewing, but that's all that I remember.

We didn't spend that much time at Grandmother's. She was an excellent cook. I can't say I follow in that track at all.

What about your grandfather?

He was more easily going. The thing that stands out in my mind about him was that he would come up and spend the summers at our house. He used to love to do things with us and he loved to go shopping. He would say "Just drop me off in the shoe department, no hurry. I'll just sit there and watch the circus go by."

Margaret Goodner McFadden c. 1920

I know the one disappointment that I had where Grandmother showed her will and of course, Granddaddy too. But she didn't wait for him to make the decision. She made it right then and there. They had a man working on the farm and he would bring supplies in from the farm for their use in the kitchen. He asked me if I would like to ride back to the farm. Margaret was out there. I thought it would be an interesting ride to go in a horse and buggy with those supplies. But my grandmother wouldn't let me because she said he sometimes wets his pants [laughs]. He doesn't have the control that he should have and she was afraid that this would happen while I was riding with him. But that's the only thing I remember. I thought "Well, gee, he can hold it for that long." I made excuses for him in my mind, but I was young. I must have been about eight or nine, something like that and I wanted to go out to the farm.

How old do you think he was?

I'm guessing. I would say in his forties. That's a real guess though. I guess that's all as far as Grandmother and Granddaddy are concerned.

What do you know about their values, philosophies and religious beliefs?

They were definitely Protestant. But I don't think they went to church every Sunday. Farmers, you know, they always had excuses if they didn't want to do something. As far as values are concerned they were very strong-willed in their beliefs and their desires. It's hard to say. I never went to church with them. I went to church with Margaret and Mac. But they went to the Episcopalian Church.

Was that because of Margaret or Mac?

Margaret, I would say. I don't know. It could have been one as equally strong in their beliefs, but I need to stick to the subject. One thing I remember about going to church. It was in the Episcopalian Church. Margaret bought me a new dress and she bought me my first brassiere. I felt like a queen with all those pretty things. They were peach color. Until then I'd always had hand-me-downs or something like that. But my dad did not work through the depression and he had some hard times in that respect.

How old were you when you got that dress?

I was thirteen, I think. She had a big police dog and he would jump and he scared people. But he was very good with me. He was very kind

Elizabeth age 13 with new dress, bra and dog

and made me feel very important because other people were afraid of him, but he was very nice to me.

My mother's youngest sister, Sarah, married a fellow that had been in the navy. Karl Reber was his name. They were down to Grandmother's at the same time we were that particular summer. I was about ten, something like that when this happened. He smoked and I guess he just didn't like me. He was smoking and he told me to come and sit on his lap. So I did and he said "Now you watch my eyes and I will inhale from the cigarette, but the smoke will come out my eyes". And he said "Now you watch my eyes and don't take your eyes away from mine". So I was diligently paying attention thinking the smoke was going to come out his eyes. But what he did was with his cigarette he burned my hand intentionally. It was quite a deep burn. I told my mother. I didn't tell my dad, but I told my mother. She said "Well, we're at Grandmother's house and we don't want to cause a problem at somebody else's house". So I felt like she didn't believe me that he would do something like that on purpose.

When your uncle burned your hand, what did you do? Did you scream?

No, I was in somebody else's house and you didn't do those things. I ran to my mother. She said "We're in somebody else's house and I can't make a fuss and he probably did it by accident". That wasn't true, but that's what she wanted to believe. That's what she wanted me to believe to save trouble.

What was his reaction?

He laughed.

I liked Margaret a lot, but I didn't particularly like Mac. I was thirteen. It was the summer I went down there as a graduation from grade school gift and I went on the Greyhound bus. Because I was a junior, the bus driver was put in charge of me. That's the trip where I stopped the bus. I told you about that.

When Buford, my mother's oldest brother saw me (he called me Libby) he said "Libby, you look like the flies have been sittin' all over your face." That's because I had freckles. Brian had freckles a lot when he was young too. So he inherited that tendency from me, also. But anyway, back to Mac. When he said hello he put his arms around me and gave me a kiss. But it wasn't a natural kiss. It was a

French kiss and Margaret wasn't in the room. He just took advantage and that's why I never liked him.

Goodner family c. 1931 - Back row: Bufford Goodner, "Mac" McFadden, Margaret McFadden, Francis Geren, Tella Radcliffe, Clarence Radcliffe, Sarah Goodner - Front row (seated): Drucilla Goodner, Elizabeth Radcliffe, Marion Radcliffe, Katherine Goodner Geren, Harold "Bucky" Geren, Priscilla Radcliffe, Virginia Radcliffe, Gerome Lee Goodner, Ada Mae Goodner.

Buford, Mother's oldest brother, he liked Marion because she loved to read. She was always off in a corner reading anything she could get her hands on. He took the National Geographic and he kept them all in his bedroom. I couldn't even go in the door. He wouldn't let me look at the magazines or anything at all. But Marion could come in anytime she wanted to, but he liked Marion. Mother's youngest brother, Gerome Lee, they always called him GL, I was his favorite. I remember a doll that he sent me for Christmas, Drusilla. I named it after his wife. Her name was Drusilla. I didn't particularly like her, but I couldn't say anything against her. She had a voice I didn't particularly care for, one of those piercing voices and she was always getting after GL for one reason or another. But he sent me this beautiful doll and my sisters didn't get anything from him.

I'm wandering through my mother's family. Buford was the oldest son and my mother was the oldest daughter and the next boy was GL. As far as the girls are concerned, after Mother came Margaret, I think and then Katie. I think that's it.

And Sarah?

Sarah was the youngest, yes. She died when she was 39 from lupus, but they didn't know what it was back then. That mean uncle that burned my hand was her husband.

After she died did you ever see him again?

No and Mother always thought that he ran around beforehand. He didn't come home at night, a lot...things like that.

What kind of work did your mother's parents do?

They had the farm and I've forgotten how many acres. There was a couple hundred, at least. So they had the farm and they raised animals and a lot of things that come with the farm.

Did they just use that farm to support themselves or did they sell some of the food to other people?

I don't remember that. I know they sold it. They took care of my great grandfather which was my grandmother's dad. He outlived his wife. She was ninety-some years old and she still rode a horse when she was living. She must have been around ninety-four, ninety-five when she died. They took care of him with all their needs and so forth. The children, they all reaped the harvest, you might say. Katie, she was selfish when it came to making money. I know she was the next to the last one living. Margaret was still living when Katie died.

Katie died after your mother died?

No, because what Katie did when they sold the farm…I don't remember what they sold it for, but they got a good price for it and Katie was in charge. She gave her brothers and sisters $5,000 a piece because she said that she deserved everything else because she had taken care of the father after the mother died.

This would be your grandfather that she took care of?

Yes, so that she felt that she deserved everything else and she got a lot. But she made enemies with family the way that she handled it, the selfish way.

But it's funny when you compare our family, the four girls and then the aunts and uncles on my mother's side. Of course, we were never very close with my dad's side. They didn't speak for years. Now as far as Virginia's concerned, I think she inherited more of Katie's ways when it comes to money. Marion, she was studious. She was always studious. She went through college and never bought a book. She went to Wayne University and she just walked down to the library and used their books all through school. She had, you might say, a photographic memory and so she would take notes. She graduated with honors.

Priscilla, I don't know who she is like, but if she had two pennies she gave it away. I think because she was so heavy. That started when she was married to Willard because he ran around. She took care of the children, raised the children, you might say and if she had two cents she would…I always felt like she was trying to buy love from other people by doing that.

But as far as I'm concerned, I don't know. I probably resemble Margaret more than any of the others. I don't know. But she was a little strong-willed too [laughs]. But she was a good person, though and she gave of herself.

As far as Margaret and Mac were concerned...we were talking about the church and how they went to the Episcopalian Church. So they would take me there and that's where I was invited to go to an ice cream social at the church, back in those days. I was invited by the grandson of the original JC Penney. But I left after I had some ice cream and walked home because he was very egotistical. Because his grandfather was who he was he thought he was untouchable. The friends should flock to him because of his position and his grandfather.

How old were you guys then?

That was the summer that I was thirteen.

So even at that age he was acting like that?

Well, I felt like he was so wrapped up in himself and he was fluttering around with all the girls and everything and so it was almost like I wasn't there with anybody. I just felt that I wasn't having a good time so I walked home to Margaret's.

Did you ever hear from him again?

Nope. No.

What else would you like to say about your mother's parents?

I don't know a great deal. Granddaddy was always very warm and he always made you feel like you were important to him. He made everybody feel that way. She was more standoffish. She was ill a great deal. I think, I don't know for sure, but I think she had sugar diabetes. She lost her sight. She was heavy.

But nobody knows what was wrong with her, or you just can't remember?

Well, I was young enough when she died that I wouldn't remember.

How old were you when she died?

Oh, about five or six.

[Addriene "Ada" Mae Fullbright Goodner died in November 10, 1955 when Elizabeth was 31 years old.]

Really? This was your grandmother?

Yes, my mother's mother.

When your mother had the nervous breakdown, was this the lady that came to Michigan?

Yes.

So you were younger than I thought. For some reason I thought you said you were seventeen. So you were younger then?

I was about seventeen when Granddaddy died. We used to go to Montgomery Ward and he loved to go along. I think Montgomery Ward, it seems to me they operate to some degree in some states yet. But I don't know, the same as Federal's. I thought Federal's went bankrupt and yet I have seen where they still operate in some states.

[Gerome Lee Goodner died in November 1, 1959 when Elizabeth was 35 years old.]

Your mother had a nervous breakdown when you were a lot smaller than you said last week?

Yes, I must have been. Grandmother must have been older than I was thinking too. She must have died when I was thirteen or fourteen. I would say fourteen.

The summer that you went there on the bus she was still alive?

Yes, and I was thirteen because that was my birthday gift from the good Lord [laughs]. He decided I was physically a woman at that stage [laughs].

Oh, goodness, that must have been a fun bus ride.

Well, and on my birthday too.

Now we're going to talk about your father's family a little bit, whatever you know about them. Where and when were your father's mother and father born?

I think it would be in that book.

Wasn't that about your mother's family, though?

Yes. But when they break down the family, you know so and so married so and so and begat so and so.

Okay, so it's in there?

I should think it would be.

[William Clarence Ratcliff was born June 27, 1897 in Cleveland, Tennesse. Tella Jane Goodner was born August 22, 1899 in Cleveland, Tennesse. William Clarence Radcliffe (note name change) and Tella Jane Goodner were married March 9, 1918]

Okay, I'll get that and I'll look. Do you remember his mother's maiden name?

No. Did I tell you Mother's mother's maiden name? It was, oh, gosh... I know it too. It was something like Brightmore.

[Elizabeth is referring to her grandmother, Ada Mae Fullbright.]

Fullbright?

Yes, that's it, Fullbright. Yes, it's in the computer. Howard did tracing, you know. He had pictures of that side of the family.

Ratclif family c 1933 - Back row (standing): Marion Radcliffe, Clarence Radcliffe, Tella Radcliffe, Virginia Radcliffe, Vernon Shanklin, Cecile Ratcliff Shanklin, Robert Shanklin, Letha Ratcliff Spicer, Walter Spicer, Front row (sitting): James Henry Ratcliff, Priscilla Radcliffe, Elizabeth Radcliffe, Jimmie Spicer, Amanda Ratcliff

But the first time I saw him, Granddaddy Ratcliff...there's a picture. I think Howard's got a copy of it too. I was fairly young. We were all lined up. It was Daddy's sisters and their family and then Daddy and his family and so forth. He had two sisters. One was Letha and the other one was Cecile. Cecile is...Mother never liked Cecile. Whenever she got mad at Marion she would say "You're just like Cecile [laughs]!" I don't remember who she compared me with, but I know she...I always got the job of mopping the floors and if something fell down the toilet even though it was dirty in there then I had to fish down and get it. I had the dirty jobs.

Marion was ill a lot when she was young. I can remember her laying and crying and the terrible ear aches. They operated on the ears.

They told her when she went in the service that her eardrums were so scarred from the operations from when she was young that she could be someplace where there's a lot of bang, a lot of noise and it would cause her to go deaf. That's what happened. She was in Germany and in Neuschwanstein and I don't know what it was that made the noise. But her hearing, just like that, it went.

In one ear or both?

Both, yes. I can remember her crying terribly.

When Priscilla was a member of the family... Mother, she didn't have a washing machine. She washed everything in the bathtub on a scrub board and she didn't have it easy. We were always dressed in white. And...but I've forgotten where I was leading to.

You were talking about when your mother got mad at Marion she always called her Cecile.

Yes and I always had to scrub all the floors and so forth. Even after I was married I scrubbed every room in that house and there were eight rooms in that house.

Which house?

The one on Asbury Park.

The one you grew up in?

Yes, well from the time I was thirteen.

You still went back there after you were married and scrubbed the floors?

No. I scrubbed the ceilings and the walls in all the rooms. They hadn't been done in several years so she asked me if I would do them all. As a gift for doing it, I have a little gold cross that has a little tiny diamond in the center...a chip like. But I've got it in here.

Your mother gave you that for doing that?

Yes. Mother was a saver and she did. Like when Howard was little and Brian was a baby and he was crawling. It was on bare floors because we didn't have any rugs. This one day Mother took me to a place where they had odd pieces of rugs. It was a real deep pile, very good quality, excellent quality. It was a 9x11. They used to be strictly 8x10, 9x12, so forth. This had never sold and I know Mother paid $55 for that piece. I had it for years. I still had it in the basement of the Brighton house.

She bought me my first washing machine. It was a Maytag. I never had a washing machine before that. I had to take it to the laundromat or something like that. It's funny I don't remember too much. We lived in Highland Park in a flat at that time. I don't remember exactly where I took those things to wash them. That's funny. Brian was a baby so I certainly had to do a lot of washing. There was no such thing as diapers you could throw away.

She did a lot of good things for me after I was married. They loaned us, through Mother...Mother insisted that Daddy take out this mortgage on their house to loan it to us so that we'd have enough money to make a down payment on the Northville house. We were supposed to pay it back. I think it was $40 a month. I don't know how that was handled. I know through a bank. Daddy didn't have...he worked for the school system. Mother was the saver, as I said. I know it sure

Tella Jane Radcliffe c 1929

helped me.

I remember when the kids got the mumps and I got them through the kids. Mother had never had them so she wouldn't come in the house. But she brought over bags of groceries for us and sat them on the porch and tapped on the window and talked to me through the window. She didn't have to do that. But Frank was working.

That was what made me mad...one of the many things. Frank, he would be a month behind in making the payment so that Daddy had to make the payment. He would say "Well, he knows he'll get it." I always believed in paying things on time and particularly, you don't take advantage of relatives. Sometimes he was two months behind and he'd say, "Well, he knows he'll get it." He was playing with Katie at that point too so that made it worse [laughs].

And you knew that then?

Yes. I used to dream of having enough money to take the kids and move to New Zealand. That was my dream [laughs].

Why New Zealand?

It was as far away as I could think of to get away from him [laughs]. There are some things you shouldn't put in the book [laughs].

And why not?

I have to let you be the judge there.

You need to be the judge. Have you inherited any of your father's side of the family's characteristics?

No. No and I can't say my father did either.

Do you think that you just don't know what kind of people they were?

I know what my dad told us. When he was young, how he was treated. He used to sing at the church.

Your grandfather or your father sang at the church?

My father...that wax cylinder I told you about, that was the song on there that he sang for his mother at her request when she was dying. But his father...nobody ever liked his father because I think they knew he was running around and stuff. I know Daddy told one year that when he was in... I can't say...high school, middle school? They took his father's buggy all apart and put it up on top of the barn and put it together again. Of course, I'm sure he had to take it down. He didn't say that. But he says he really enjoyed doing that [laughs].

His father sent him to... he said it was like a boy's orphanage. They really mistreated the boys that were there. They were also teaching them the bible so that when they left there they were ordained ministers. But the only time that he ever... after the war he was sent to Lynch, Kentucky, which was the poorest area of the United States at that time. It's still poor, but it's a long way from what it was. It's a beautiful area. The church supplied springs, not box springs, but the old fashioned springs and then a very tired mattress that sat on the floor. In the kitchen there was a stove that you built and cooked on wood. There was a table that two people could sit at for meals. That's all the furniture that there was in the house. Virginia was born on that mattress and springs on the floor.

This was the house that your parents lived in when they were first married?

No, when he came back from the war. Then he was assigned because they needed a minister so they sent him. He didn't like many things about the church. He didn't believe in passing the collection plate because people were so poor. They just couldn't put anything in it. Once in a while someone would put a chicken in there or something. How they got out of that area was he told them he was leaving the church. He got a job at the mines as a bookkeeper. So that's how he made enough money to get to Detroit, barely.

Was Marion born in Detroit too? Was Virginia the only one that wasn't?

No, Virginia is the only one that was.

Virginia was the only one born in Detroit?

No, Lynch, Kentucky. Marion was born in Dearborn. I was born in Detroit and so was Priscilla.

They wouldn't have had the house on Asbury Park if it wasn't for my mother being such a saver. I remember she used to can. Boy, did she can. She did hundreds of jars of different things to last through the winter. She had a garden she used to grow.

You had a garden?

Mother did.

Did you ever garden after you left home?

I had one in Brighton, but I didn't put the time in that you should.

You didn't have one when your kids were small?

No. When they lived in Dearborn, that's where Daddy would meet and talk with Henry Ford, the original, the father. They used to get their hair cut at the same place...ten cents.

Daddy used to enjoy telling about the time...I remember the gun and Daddy got rid of it. He had this gun for Mother for protection because he was working nights. I don't know where he was working at that point, but it was Christmas Eve and he had ordered some groceries to be delivered. They didn't charge for delivery and he bought some groceries and they were to deliver them because he was on his way to work and he couldn't do it. The delivery boy had so many deliveries he didn't get there until almost midnight. Mother didn't think anybody was coming at that hour and it couldn't be anything but robbery. So she got the gun and she shot right through the door and she barely missed him. He dropped the groceries and ran. That's why Daddy got rid of the gun. He said that she got too nervous and she was lucky she didn't commit murder.

From there they bought a house on St. Mary's. I think they paid $3,000 for that house. It was during the depression. It was just before the depression that they bought the house and Daddy lost his job. When he lost his job, what he did until he could find work, he hired an Indian and he would do anything for meals. Mother always had someone coming to the door. Even if it was nothing more than half an open-face sandwich or peanut butter, she would always give them something. Not for work, but just because they were hungry. She never refused anybody something to eat.

But this Indian, all he wanted...but I think Daddy paid him more, paid him other than just meals. The two of them built a structure to raise the house, to hold it up so they could put a basement under it. So they ended up having a full basement down there. We had a lot of pleasure down there. He made a good sized workshop that he kept locked. There was a full kitchen down there for summertime when it was so hot, otherwise. They would eat down there, can down there. I hated canning peaches because I was young and it would make your arms itch. I would be itchy all the way out to my body, I think. I'm wandering around...the schizos!

July 7, 2010

Has your mother shared any stories she knew about her parent's childhood?

The only things I remember at all are some things she obviously learned as a child, which was making butter, as an example...household things.

Where and when was your mother born?

Mother was born in 1899 and she was born in Cleveland, Tennessee on August 22.

Where did she grow up?

In Cleveland, Tennessee.

And her maiden name was?

Goodner. As I understand it, every person in the United States, according to that book (Goodner book) is related to a single marriage that came over to the United States. Which is unusual and that's why the book is in the Library of Congress.

You mean every Goodner?

Yes.

Tell about the family in which your mother grew up. Do you know what her childhood was like?

I remember learning what girls should do as they grow up and marry and so forth. I remember Mother telling me, as an example, that the first thing you should do when you get up is make the bed because it's the largest item in the room and if you make the bed first at least the room looks a lot tidier than if it were left unmade. Things like that.

I also remember how she had just taken a bath and she had a towel wrapped around her. Daddy was a friend of GL's. I think it was GL he was a friend of. He came over to the house. They went upstairs to GL's bedroom just as Mother walked out of the bathroom that was upstairs. She was so embarrassed that she grabbed the towel and put it over her head hoping Daddy wouldn't realize which one she was.

Tella Jane Radcliffe c 1922

But he knew? Oh, heavens, yes!

He also told me once, with a big smile on his face, I don't know what brought it up. He told me that he had to educate Mother after they were married because she was so small that she hadn't started to menstruate yet and he had to tell her all about it. Because being small they didn't say anything about those things back then until it was maturity. That's really all I remember.

What memories do you have of your mother during your childhood?

She was a disciplinarian. She sort of ran the house. She was also the saver and I firmly believe that we wouldn't have had the things that we had, had it not been for Mother being such a saver.

I also remember that being the disciplinarian, Virginia being five and a half years older than I, she always got out of things because she said she had to practice the piano. Marion of course was obviously ill a great deal the time. Her ear problems were quite severe to the point that they were operated on and it damaged her ear drums so badly that eventually it caused her to go deaf. They didn't know how to do things back then the way they do today.

Virginia managed to get out of so much that I had to scrub the floors. Once in a while I had to put socks on and polish the floors because Mother always waxed them after they were scrubbed. If she didn't think I did a good job scrubbing I had to do it all over again. I had to scrub the bathroom. If something fell down into the toilet, even though the toilet had been used, I was the one that had to fish it out. I felt that I got all the dirty chores and so I was sure that

The Radcliffe girls in 1933 - Elizabeth, Marion, Priscilla, Tulla, Virginia

Mother did not like me. After all, I had been told by so many people, "You must be adopted because you don't look at all like your sisters." For years and years I believed it until I was old enough to remember Margaret and what she looked like. Virginia had a lot of clever privileges. Marion did strictly from illness.

Back in those days they had a room at school and the school system where the child was not healthy or they felt that it wasn't fed properly so that's why it wasn't healthy. That wasn't true in Marion's case. It was strictly from illnesses. She was so little. Marion has always been little. So that left me. When Priscilla came in, that made a fourth child and a lot of work for Mother, because she scrubbed out the clothes in the bathtub on a wash board. I used to have to scrub out Priscilla's diapers after she had messed them and empty them out in the toilet and then scrub them out in the bathtub.

How much older were you than Priscilla?

Five years. Priscilla was extremely spoiled because she was such a very pretty little child. She liked to have me take care of her and if I didn't she would, as Mother used to say "She'll squall". She didn't say cry; squall was the word they used back then. I had to take care of Priscilla a great deal, which limited me on friendships and any number of things.

I remember the people next door had a...I don't know how old she was, but she was small. I would guess she was two or three years of age. They put her on the front porch with a gate to keep her from going down the stairs. But there was a banister that she could get through. One day she crawled through the banister and fell about three feet down. She wasn't hurt, but she sure screamed. Mother was sewing. She made all of our clothes. She was sewing and I was crying because the man had hit me and there had been quite a squabble as a result. I remember crying and I cried just as long as I could possibly make the tears flow because I was sitting at Mother's knees on the floor. Mother was sitting on a chair. Mother was consoling me because the man had hit me. I was innocent of anything I had been accused of. He said she couldn't get off so I must have pushed her off. I cried until I couldn't possibly cry any longer strictly because I was getting this warm loving attention from Mother.

Our parents, it's true of all parents of that age, it seems, at least in the South. I don't know how it was up North. They learned their ways in the South. Mother was never a loving person. Never...and Daddy wasn't either. She bossed him so much that I think he avoided being home as much as possible. He had to ride the street car to get to work and it took a lot of time. Where he worked was Detroit City Ice and Fuel Company that was on the other side of the city. He had to transfer and everything.

In high school I think that's why I became a majorette. I was the top one. In fact, I appeared with Woody Herman's band at Michigan Theater at a contest for all of the majorettes and drum majors in the state. I came in second because I was afraid. Although I was extremely fast, I came in second. The person that came in first was a boy to start with. The glaring lights that they put on you, they shone right into my eyes so I didn't do any aerial work with the baton because I was afraid I wouldn't catch it with the light shining in my eyes. Apparently, it didn't affect him that much and he won, but I came in second in the state.

Elizabeth as Cooley High School Majorette

In high school I had a music teacher that had roaming hands and I would never...I would make sure that I never went with him by myself ever again. He told me to come into practice, that I wasn't raising my knees high enough. He wanted to help me in that area, he said. Well, he wanted to help me alright [laughs].

We used to fill the auditorium and the auditorium was about four times the size of the one up in Snowflake... about four times as large. *[The Snowflake auditorium seats approximately 800.]* We filled it. Parents really came out because we did put on a big production. He wanted me to come out during this one piece that the orchestra played and play credenzas on the piano in a certain area where it's written into the music. When I came out, everybody thought I was going to do a big concerto or something, I'm sure. I did a good job on what I was told to do. The rest of the time I played in the orchestra.

I was aged sixteen when I auditioned for the All City A Orchestra. They had an A and B orchestra. I auditioned on that to play with the Detroit Symphony for one concert, which I did. I was picked. It scared me to death, but I did it.

I met Frank in high school. I think when being raised in a family that was not demonstrative...your parents didn't put their arms around you. My mother never told me that she loved me until just before she died [crying]. She said also that she would live longer if I would take care of her. But she would not change herself. We had tried to get her to come and live with us, but she wouldn't do it. The world had to change to suit her.

Frank Jones - high school sweetheart and first husband

Frank, he was so possessive...extremely possessive. It made me feel like I was important...that I was loved. But it wasn't that. It was just like he said, "I can't relax unless I'm in control of everything around me." He said that when we were in divorce court. I told him he'd feel better and life would be easier if he learned to relax and that was his answer. Boy, how true it was. So I made a mistake in marrying too young for the wrong reason. But I didn't realize it was the wrong reason [laughs].

How old were you?

Nineteen. Then he stalled on the divorce because he didn't want to lose the house so he stalled it for two years. During that two years, I met John. He was an angel in comparison [crying].

Describe your mother's work both in and out of the home.

She never worked out of the home. She sang in the church choir for years. She played the piano, but strictly for her own pleasure. I'll never forget that song *The Star of the Sea*. She practiced that till she had it perfect. In the house she raised four girls.

Virginia was smart and she was very active in the music world. She was outstanding in Mother's eyes and she was. She graduated summa cum-laude. Marion did also. She played in the band and the orchestra. She hated it, but she did it. She played clarinet. She had a violin and until the day she died she said the happiest day of her life was when it was stolen [laughs]. She was very academic and you have to be more than just academic all A's to be summa cum-laude. But she did. She did it on her excellent record.

And then along came Elizabeth. She didn't overly strive in the academic area. She was thinking of boys and my academic bit was in the music department also and also the drum majorette bit. I don't know who's got that picture of me in my costume. Somebody's got it.

Elizabeth (second from left) and the Cooley High majors

You mean one of your children has a picture of you in a costume?

Must be. I would say it was...I don't know. Tella took so much. After Mother died, even before she died Priscilla was going through all of her things taking pictures and things that she wanted to make sure that she got them.

Priscilla was quite a chore. She was sixteen when she had to get married. Virginia was twenty or twenty-one, twenty. She graduated from high school at sixteen and that was a year ahead of time. Virginia was I think twenty or twenty-one when she had to get married. Marion and I were the only two that didn't have to get married [laughs]...two of the four [laughs]. I was almost twenty-three when I had Howard.

I used to walk home from school which was two miles. I was given five cents for bus fare. That's what it cost on the bus then for students. Instead of doing that, I walked the two miles just to buy a fudge sickle [laughs].

Do you remember what your mother's hobbies were and what she did for fun?

Singing in the church choir for the Methodist Church. She did a lot of things that a lot of mothers wouldn't do. At the time that I started playing the cello she got the cello at J.L. Hudson Company. It was thirty five dollars and she had to pay for it on time. She saved and paid for it. She couldn't pay for lessons so we walked almost three miles...I'd say it was a good three miles each way. Priscilla was in the buggy. She was two years old, but she couldn't walk that far. She'd be too tired. In the summer they gave free lessons, the Board of Education did. I'm not sure if it was the Board of Education or the City of Detroit sponsored it as a summer program. But we walked that three miles each way and laid the cello across the foot of the buggy that Priscilla was riding in. We all walked three miles each way there and then again coming home so that we could have free lessons.

Then when Mother was able to do it, save and pay for it on a regular basis she paid for Virginia to have piano lessons. Virginia was a good pianist and violinist. She bought a good violin that Bill has, Mother did for Virginia. Marion used the clarinets that Daddy used, upstairs at your place. They used the "C" clarinet all the time then. And, of course, I had the cello.

[The clarinets to which she refers were played by her father when he played with John Philip Sousa's band around the time of World War I. After Elizabeth's death, the clarinets were donated to the Musical Instrument Museum in Phoenix, Arizona and are now part of the John Philip Sousa exhibit.]

Whose idea was it for you to play the cello? Did you want to play it or did your mother want you to play it?

No, Mother decided because we had kind of a family orchestra. We played at church periodically, at different churches around. Daddy played the clarinet. Mother played the piano, Virginia first violin, Marion second violin and then you had to have a cello. But I enjoyed it except I didn't feel very feminine sitting there with your legs apart [laughs]. But I was young so it didn't matter [laughs].

The family orchestra 1934 - Marion, Elizabeth and Virginia

Which of your mother's physical and personality characteristics did you inherit?

The color of her hair [laughs]. Nope, Virginia got her good legs. Mother was small and Marion was very petite...always was. Priscilla could do no wrong and boy, she did a lot of it. I think she needed a psychiatrist. But you didn't recognize those facts to yourself let alone anyone else. Psychiatry was more or less fairly new. That's all that I can say I inherited of Mother's.

Describe her best qualities.

Perseverance.

Describe your mother's traits with which you are least compatible.

Domineering…she was domineering. She got what she wanted. She managed to do that. She worked hard.

Did she experience much sadness or tragedy when you were little?

She lost her sister…her youngest sister and also my favorite uncle. He had been in the war and he suffered so badly from arthritis. He was in the navy and the moisture in the air fed the arthritis. They gave him the choice, the Veteran's hospital. All they could do for him was to operate on him and freeze his spine. He had the choice of choosing whether he wanted to sit for the rest of his life or stand for the rest of his life. He committed suicide.

Which brother was this?

Gerome Lee, GL we called him. I was his favorite.

How did your mother deal with those tragedies?

Her mother died when I was quite young…not real young. She did it in a silent way and how can I say? She never talked about it. She didn't talk about it at all.

GL was her favorite too [laughs]. I remember the Thanksgiving that he came and stayed with us. He loved Mother's lemon pies. She could make wonderful lemon pies. So she made him one. He grabbed it and he was joking and said he was going to eat it all himself. Mother was chasing him to get him to put it down…all in fun. She was enjoying it. She was laughing. They were both laughing as they chased each other. He accidentally dropped the pie. So we scooped it up and we ate it [laughs].

What is the happiest memory of your mother?

She took us places like the Ford Sunday Evening Hour. My dad took me once. But Mother had gotten the tickets and then she got sick...a cold...so Daddy took me. Every week we used to go to the Ford Sunday Evening Hour Symphony. It was all Mother's doing to get those tickets.

In the summer time she would take us out to a park. I didn't participate, but Virginia did. They had an orchestra that played out there. It was a summer extension of the All City Orchestra. She played while we had a picnic and waited for the orchestra to be over with. I used to enjoy that picnic.

I remember Mother and her sewing machine. She was a good seamstress. The hat disappeared. I may still have that. I should give it to you to go with the book. I'm going to look for it. A little rubber doll that I got for Christmas. We had gone south that Christmas. Mother assured us that Santa Claus would have found our house and where we lived. When we

Doll dress and slip made by Elizabeth's mother in 1927. The designs on the collar are less than a quarter inch across.

got home there this little rubber doll. It's too bad it was rubber because it wouldn't have deteriorated. But it did. She made all of its clothes. They were all embroidered with French felt seams. The shoes, the booties are lost I think, unless I gave it to Virginia and that would have been stupid of me. I'm going to check. I still have the dress and the under-slip. There was a Teddy and there was a bonnet and they all matched...crepe de chine silk which is hard to sew on. She did it all by hand. I'm going to look for that because you could put it with the book. I don't know why I would have given it to her. She takes things and then gives them to Bill's wife. She rents a booth at one of those shows where they sell things. She would sell antiques and stuff too. I'm going to check. I'll let you know. It was all antique with flat French felt seams with tiny, tiny work. It was embroidered in blue with little tiny lace all along and it had the feather stitches in blue. I loved that doll, but it deteriorated with age.

What is most painful memory you have of your mother?

She and Daddy stood up for when Frank and I got married. It's hard to say. I guess the fact that I had to reach in the toilet and do things like that [laughs]. I got the dirty jobs. I really can't think of any one thing. I can't single out any one thing, really. As I look back, it's the fact that we weren't raised in a loving family. But then that's the way they were raised. So it wasn't that she didn't care because she did, but it was never shown. She went to our concerts. Daddy never went to our concerts at Cooley. Mother always went. Other than that I can't think of anything....one single thing.

She bought me the rug that we had. I lived on bare floors with Howard. When I had Brian he was crawling on a bare floor downstairs in a flat that we rented in Highland Park. It was beautiful material and plush. She bought me my first washing machine after Brian was born so I wouldn't have to scrub out diapers by hand. It was the best of the line as far as the Maytag's were concerned. I remember that well. I was so grateful.

When the kids got mumps, Brian got them. Then Howard got them. Jeff wasn't born yet. I was expecting. I caught the mumps from my children. Mother had never had them. She bought us groceries and everything. Frank never said thank you. He never thanked them for taking a mortgage on their house for us or anything that he didn't pay on time. I really can't think of one single thing. I can think of when I was older a lot of good things. But as a very young child I had to scrub the floors and do the dirty jobs, as I put it. I'm sorry I can't come up with any one thing.

children. Matt smiled at them, then turned. She thought he'd never stop overwhelming them over one drink or... When he left she leaned on the... ...as she greeted... their house...

July 13, 2010

Back tracking a little bit, I thought it might be interesting about the story for Marion and me. Marion was seven and I was five. We were playing in the back yard on a homemade teeter totter. Mother called us and we didn't get off the usual way. Marion did it on purpose. She said she was sorry. She got up real quick so that it bounced on the ground on my side and my hand was under it. I broke every bone in my left wrist. I had started school... kindergarten. I hated it because I was about a head taller than everybody else. So I would stand on the other side of the room. The door had glass in it. I would stand on the other side of the room so people looking in the door wouldn't see me and think I was dumb. I missed school as a result, for the rest of the year which made me happy. In the meantime, I stopped growing and I caught up with the kids in school...that is growth wise. By the time I started first grade we were all about the same, close to the same height. So that was a bad thing that happened, but it turned out to be good in my eyes.

Now as far as Mother's concerned...nice things she always did. Every year she would pack a picnic lunch and we would take a big basket and take the street car over to Bell Isle, which is a large island over off of downtown Detroit. Sometimes, very often, we would have a picnic there and not go to anything special. As a rule, we would go over there with a picnic lunch, all of us, on the street car and have a picnic lunch at the Scott Fountain and at the Flower House. I'm sure you remember the Flower House. San Francisco has a marvelous one. That was a couple of very nice things Mother did every year. We enjoyed it very much. After eating we were allowed to get on the regular, what they called a cradle swing. It was shaped like a cradle, but you couldn't go real high like you could with a regular swing. It was very enjoyable though. As a rule, I didn't miss the regular swing. Mother thought they were a bit dangerous because there were usually boys over there to see how high they could push things.

Tell me about your mother's spiritual and religious beliefs.

She went to the Methodist Church. Daddy was brought up in the Methodist Church. He was an ordained minister in the Methodist Church, although he only practiced it once. She sang in the choir every week and on Wednesdays she went to choir practice and we went to the show. She would pick us up after the show. That's where I saw the first Frankenstein picture. It was all in green color. Everything was green in my memory. I got very sick. I was in the lady's room throwing up and they called Mother from practice. They thought she should come and get me, which she did. I never did see the end of the movie, but I was certainly frightened. For a long time, I had nightmares about everything being green. Sometimes Frankenstein was included, but very often it was just any horror pictures, but it was all in green.

How and when did your mother die?

I'll have to look that up.

[Tella Jane Goodner Radcliffe diedDecember 15, 1986.]

How did she die?

Very miserably. She suffered terribly with arthritis. She was in a great deal of pain. She was bedridden for some time. She had gone blind. The way we understood it she had glaucoma to start with and then she ended up with macular degeneration which caused her to be totally blind. She lived alone and she was afraid to get up and walk around. She hurt so much. I remember her feet. That stands out in my mind. Her feet were so deformed. Of course, the other things were too, but that's what stands out in my mind. They were so deformed from arthritis I wondered how she could step on them let alone put shoes on.

Priscilla, when she was divorced...I never even told Mother that I was getting divorced because Virginia was getting a divorce and also Priscilla. I thought that she didn't need the knowledge of mine to make her emotional burden any greater. So I didn't say anything. Priscilla came, because she didn't have a home or anything. She didn't have any money. She would spend it as fast as she got it...literally. She tried to buy love with money with her children.

I had moved to Charlevoix the year before, John and I had. All she did was complain about Mother. Then Mother would complain that Priscilla was gone all the time and she hired a woman to come in and take care of her. The woman sat and read all the time. She didn't really take care of Mother. The last letter I got was a complaint from Priscilla saying that she would stay with Mother until March. This was in November. After March I would have to get somebody else to look after Mother as if I was the only girl in the family. I was the only one in Michigan so I might just as well have been the only girl in the family. When I lived down state I took care of Mother the whole time I was down there, several years. Shopped for her, took her places, took her to the doctor... took her everywhere before she went blind. I didn't like the letter Priscilla sent, the way she worded it. As it was, Mother died ten days before Christmas. That much I remember.

What did she actually die from?

Her heart gave out.

Where is she buried?

Acacia Park. That's where Daddy is and where Marion's ashes are and mine will be. It's all paid for. Marion paid for it to make sure because Virginia is going to be buried down in Florida with Lloyd. Priscilla had been buried at sea, in the gulf, down off of Florida.

Tella is just like her mother when it came to spending money. We gave Priscilla our inheritance, Marion and I did. Virginia gave the house and Marion and I gave the money and the house.

Marion wanted her ashes shipped and buried by Mother and Daddy and made me promise to do the same. So that's where I would like to be shipped to, after my ashes. I don't want any showing, there's no need for any thought other than the cost of the rubber container that they put you in, or it's heavy plastic, one or the other. When they came to the house to get Marion, they put her in the bag right there. She didn't want any showing or anything. That's what I want, the same thing.

What are the most important things you learned from your mother?

To follow through on commitments, for one thing. She taught me how to sew. She was a very good seamstress, very good. I made my dress to graduate from grade school. I made my dress when I graduated from high school. I, at one time was a good seamstress like Mother.

What else do you remember about her?

I remember going to the dentist with her when she was thirty some years old, about thirty five, I'm guessing. I remembered how she was dressed up in a pink sort of a satiny dress. It wasn't satin it was the pink material the doll dress was made out of. It was similar to that. I remember thinking how beautiful she was. At one time, she was. I guess you might say that covers it pretty well.

Has your father shared any stories he knew about his parents' childhoods?

No.

Not even his mother?

No.

Where and when was your father born?

He was born in Cleveland, Tennessee in 1897. Mother was born in 1899 in Cleveland, Tennessee.

William "Clarence" Ratcliff (Radcliffe) c 1902

Did he grow up in Cleveland, Tennessee?

Yes, until he was sent away. After his mother died, he was sent away. His father didn't like him.

Where was he sent?

He was sent to what was like an orphanage. They were disciplined quite severely. I remember him saying that.

Where was it, do you know?

In Athens, Tennessee. When he graduated from there he was an ordained minister. It basically was run by the Methodist Church.

How old was he when he went there?

He was sent there when his mother died, or shortly afterwards. I don't know exactly what year that was. You'll have to look in that book to see. I guess he was kind of a mischievous boy because he hated his father for the way his father treated him. I think his father treated the girls beautifully. But I also think that he took advantage of the girls physically.

[Maranda Naomi Broomfield Ratcliff died July 26, 1908.]

Why?

Because he tried to take advantage of me when I was thirteen. When I was down there, I was told to go visit him so I did. I spent the night there. He didn't do anything then. What he did was in the daytime. It was out in, like a barn. It was his garage. He kissed me and he put his hands on my bunky, as we called it, on the rear end. We used to call that the bunky. He pushed me against him so that I would feel his growth in that area.

Did you tell anybody about that?

No, huh uh. Because if I told Mother, she would have gotten furious about it and I didn't want to hurt Daddy. So I didn't for years. My mother's family was tip top, but Daddy's dad, he was known to be a lady's man. My father was as straight as a pencil.

Tell about the family in which your father grew up?

There were two girls and the one boy, Letha and Cecile. We always thought Cecile was a little bit on the funny side, on the not too smart side. Letha, she was the smarter of the two, but she was very mentally conscious of money. The last time I saw her, we stayed at her house in Gettysburg. She was always very nice. She had a boy and a girl. They both died of cancer, at a young age, really. She died of cancer, also. It was pretty strong on that side somewhere. It must have been the father, if you inherit. It must have been the father because I don't remember it ever being mentioned anybody dying of cancer on his side.

When we were there, Letha, I don't know how many times (it impressed me) that she was worried that her husband, Walter who was at least ten or fifteen years older than she was. She was worried that he would die before she did and before he was old enough to collect social security. Therefore, she would not be eligible for any when it came around. It would be umpteen years that she wouldn't be eligible for social security because of him being so much older than her. As it turned out, he lived longer than she did. He didn't worry about money. He lived a long time. He was in his nineties, I think, when he died.

[Walter Conrad Spicer was born February 25, 1888 in Laurel Springs, North Carolina and died February 17, 1972 in Fremont, California]

They were very nice. Their children were also. James, they called him Jimmy. He had the most beautiful hair. He was good looking. He had this beautiful, wavy, curly hair. He said "It's all the way you wash your hair." He washed my hair for me to show me how [laughs]. You know, we had a weird family on that side [laughs]. No wonder we didn't associate for years and years and years.

Do you know what your father's childhood was like?

Yes, his father was mean to him. After his mother died his father was very mean to him.

Was this the person who married the twin sister of his wife after his wife died?

Yes. His wish...I'm sure it was carried out, positive. His wish was that he had one sister on one side of him and the other on the other side of him in the cemetery.

Do you remember any stories your dad told about his childhood?

No, other than how he was treated mean at the orphanage type of place that he was sent to. He mentioned that several times. They worked him half to death, severe punishment, whippings if they didn't do it in the length of time they thought to be right. But other than that, he didn't mention it.

What memories do you have of your father during your childhood?

He was quiet. He would sing. He had a beautiful voice, tenor. Every now and then he would sing. For some reason or another he just stopped one day. He didn't sing anymore. I don't' know why.

How old were you when he stopped?

I'm guessing around twelve, ten or twelve.

What kind of work did your father do?

After World War One he was sent to Lynch, Kentucky. He was the minister of the Methodist Church there. The weather was so hot and humid it made him ill. He would pass out from the heat. Marion did the same thing. She would pass out from the heat.

That's where Virginia was born on an old fashioned bed spring and a well-worn cheap mattress on top of it. A wood stove in the kitchen, a kitchen table and two chairs. That was the extent of the furniture that was in the house. That's why Virginia always jokes that she was born on the floor.

He couldn't take it so he got a job as a bookkeeper for the mines that he was near. He hated the ministry because number one, the weather and number two, the fact that the people were so poor that he hated to pass a collection plate. Once in a while he would get a chicken. But other than that, they just barely got along. They were half starved. He told us how he had lived for two months on, Mother and he both, porridge, we called it. We've always called it porridge. Cliff, after having heard that story, Virginia's son, the oldest one, Cliff, he was in college and he ran out of money. Rather than ask anybody for help, he did the same thing because of Daddy's story.

From there he managed to save enough money to move up to Michigan to Dearborn. He moved up there and that's where he met Henry Ford, Sr. They took their hair cuts at the same barbershop. That's where he met Henry Ford. He used to say how they sat and talked just like ordinary people. There wasn't anything special about him at all. He treated everybody the same. He had a lot of respect for Henry Ford, Sr.

That's where Mother had groceries sent at Christmas. They said they would deliver them on Christmas Eve. They sent a boy to deliver and he had so many deliveries to make that he came to Mother's and Daddy's when Daddy wasn't home. He was working. It was close to midnight. Mother took out a gun that Daddy had bought some time or another and shot right through the door...barely missed the kid. He was delivering the groceries. She thought it must be a burglar because nobody would be delivering groceries at that hour [laughs].

See why I don't want you to have a gun [both laugh hysterically]?

I'm more stable than that. I wouldn't do that.

They rented a house on 24th Street. I have the address somewhere in that box, I think. It's in Daddy's handwriting. That's where I was born. Marion was born in Dearborn. I was born on 24th Street.

This new subdivision, these homes were built and Mother and Daddy bought one. They paid three thousand something for that house. I remember seeing papers on it when I was older. I didn't get a lot more when I resold it. Even though Daddy raised the house and finished the basement and had a big kitchen down there and a big workshop that was all closed off and a playroom. We called it a playroom because in the summer that's where we played. In the winter the furnace heated it.

I can remember Marion getting on the library table that we had down there. She'd sit there with her ear up next to the radio. Before it started she made the grids for the innings. She was an avid baseball fan. She wrote everything down. She could tell you anything about baseball before she got married. We were living at 11635 St. Mary's and that's also where Priscilla was born before the basement was put in. It's funny I can remember that house number so clearly. We moved to Asbury Park and I was thirteen. That's how we ended up at Asbury Park. That's where we lived and Mother died there. It was a nice neighborhood, very, very nice neighborhood.

[It appears Elizabeth was having a bit of confusion here. The house to which she refers, i.e., the one she sold after her mother's death, was the one on Asbury Park. This is the one where her parents lived until their deaths. The house that was "raised" seems to be the previous house, possibly the one referenced as being on St. Marys Street.]

What was he doing to work when you moved to those places?

I stopped in Lynch, Kentucky when he worked as the minister in the church. Then he saved enough to get a job as the bookkeeper in audit for the mines there. Then he moved to Dearborn. I think he was out of work at first. I'm not sure where he worked at that point. When we moved to St. Mary's, he ended up working at the Detroit City Ice and Fuel Company. From there he went to the Detroit school system. He was in charge of all the engineers. There was more than one. I've forgotten how many. Also, there were people that he had to make sure that they did the cleaning...the rooms and the halls, polishing them. They used to polish the floors every night...wash them and polish them. That's where he retired from.

What other interests did he have?

He liked to work with wood. Around home it was 'fix this and fix that' and 'do this and do that'. Mother had her list and it seemed to be never ending. He worked with wood. He liked to do that.

He took me once to the Detroit Sunday Evening Symphony, but just once. Mother took me the rest of the time.

Was it was just you and he?

Yes. You got free tickets so they only handed out so many per person, per couple or whatever. I really don't know other than that type of thing. He worked on his car when it needed help. I don't know what else he did. He built the house at the lake. That took two years. He did it all by himself, didn't have help.

He worked as an electrician between City Ice and Fuel. What did I say? Then he went to the school system. But in between there he went to school and got his license for electrical contractor. Whenever he had any time whatsoever he was out wiring houses and that type of thing. That basically was his main job before he went to Mackenzie High School as the electrician there.

What did he do for fun?

[Laughs] I don't remember. I don't remember him doing anything strictly for fun except out to the lake. He would go fishing by himself or take one of the boys, Virginia's boys with him. I don't remember anything actually, other than that, that he did for relaxation.

Which of your father's physical and personality characteristics did you inherit?

I don't know. It's hard to say. He was a hard worker. He kept his mouth shut. Whenever Mother told him to do something, he just did it. I can remember him chasing her around the house and putting his arms around her and enjoying some fun in that way. He would laugh. He didn't belong to any club or anything like that. I'll get the picture and you can look and see if you see if I look like him [laughs].

Nobody ever told you that you looked like him in a certain way when you were a child?

No. When I was young, I was always told I was adopted. I must have been adopted because everyone else was blond and blue eyed and I was…Virginia had hazel eyes and Priscilla and Marion both had very blue eyes. They inherited that from their father. The brown eyes I got from Mother's side. Really that's all I know.

Describe your father's best qualities.

He knew when to shut his mouth [laughs]. That's more than I do apparently, according to Howard. He followed through. When he'd start something, he finished it. He didn't just procrastinate and set it aside with the promise of 'I'll get back to it'. When he started something, he stuck with it until it was finished. I guess that's all right.

He was a caring person. In fact, he cared too much about some things. It was the dead of winter and he was going to be coming by Cooley High at the approximate time I would be getting off, leaving, going home. He said he would pick me up, which he did.

I think I'd better tell this story while I remember. I remember him taking me to school one morning. He wouldn't pick up anybody that I knew along the way. It was cold, winter time. About the second time that happened, I pretended like I had dropped something to pick it up. He asked me why I did that. I said because I'm embarrassed that you pass my friends up and they know his car and it embarrasses me. He said "I won't pick anybody up because I don't want people to get the wrong idea as far as I'm concerned. When I give people a ride I want them to know me before I give them a ride." And he wouldn't. I guess someone had a daughter, as I remember, that had taken a ride with a stranger. It turned out that they took advantage of her, or he did took advantage of her. He didn't want people, unless they knew him, he didn't want people to think he that he was somebody trying to pick up a school girl. I didn't feel that anybody would feel that way about my father. He was overly cautious in so many ways and that was one.

Just like the Christmas that Virginia got that two wheeled bike and he made Mother take it back. He had a friend that had a daughter that got killed on a two wheeled bike and he said he didn't want that to happen to any of his girls. He was just overly cautious that anything would happen to us. It was only because he had a friend that had lost a child as a result of this. And as a result of being picked up by a stranger, et cetera. So he insisted that he know people before he picked them up.

Whatever he did, he always followed through until it was done. He did a good job on things. He was a perfectionist in making sure it was done right. He was very definite in that way of thinking.

And you don't think you inherited that from him?

I don't see it. Do you?

Yes, look at your sewing and the other things. You like the house just perfect.

Well, it bothers me if things aren't just so when I finish them so I guess maybe that's something there.

I think it might be.

Well, you're a better judge than I am.

Not necessarily.

Yes.

Describe your father's traits with which you are least compatible.

I have to say that he showed a partiality. He had a friend RJ Only that asked him once, I overheard it, which of his girls did he favor. He said "I guess I'd have to say Virginia because she was the firstborn." That was very disillusioning to me because I tried hard to be a substitute for the fact that he didn't have a son.

I never had a favorite when my children were growing up. Howard thought so at times, I think. But he was five years old, almost five and a half years old before Brian came along…five years. I think most kids kind of twist things around to reaffirm their beliefs, or something or other. I don't know what. But in all truth I can say that I have never, when they were growing up, shown any partiality. I loved one as much as the next one. I didn't think one was any better than the other.

July 20, 2010

Describe your father's traits with which you are least compatible.

Least compatible? With which husband?

No, this is your father's traits.

I can't think of any.

I think I asked that last time and you had the same answer so you win. Did he experience much sadness or tragedy while you were little?

Not that I know of.

What is the happiest memory you have of your father?

Hearing him sing was the happiest memory.

What is the most painful memory you have of him?

There for a while before he died Mother accused him of...before he died, of being unfaithful to her. He came over to my house and he just looked so tired. He said "Your mother's been at it again. I've never been unfaithful to your mother and I never would be, but she won't believe me." I think she had been after him trying to get him to admit to something that he didn't do.

He worked for the school and had his own office. One day Mother stopped over there and one of the teachers was talking to him about something innocent about the building or something. Mother thought he had been unfaithful with her. She believed that he was unfaithful until the day he died. I'll never forget his face. He was brow beaten by this fantasy that Mother had built up in her imagination. What else can I say? He just unloaded to me.

He used to wire houses and buildings, but mostly houses. In fact he wired Ralph Boles' house and I used to go with him whenever I could. I enjoyed doing that very much. It was so cold, it was wintertime. I remember his hands were cracked and bleeding because he couldn't wear warm gloves and work with wire.

I guess the happiest time was when he took me to work with him. I enjoyed that. I was proud.

Tell about your father's spiritual or religious beliefs.

He was definitely Protestant. The only thing I ever remember him saying... he told why he left the ministry. Later on when we were older, he made the statement that it wouldn't bother him if one of his girls married out of the race, but it would hurt him and bother him if they changed religions and joined a different church than what we belonged to. The fact that we didn't belong to a church, the girls didn't... I've never belonged to a church in my life. Virginia thinks I did belong to a church. She was the church organist and the only one with church influence. Marion was gone in the service for several years. But I don't think she went to church either. She died and supposedly as an atheist.

[Elizabeth was a member of the Westminster Presbyterian Church in Detroit for a number of years in the late 1950s.]

Did your dad know she was an atheist?

I don't think so. Marion was very quiet about those things. Anything that would hurt somebody, unless she had to tell, she didn't.

Why did your father leave the church?

Because of weather and where the church sent him...to Lynch, Kentucky where Virginia was born. He asked for a transfer for health reasons and they refused. So that's when he started saving a bit of money to go north where it wouldn't be so hot.

Did he go to church when you were young and did you go with him?

When we were young, yes. Why he stopped going I don't know. I know he worked on Saturdays and Sundays wiring houses. That was his electrical time. The rest of the week was devoted to working at the school district. He never preached religion to us that I remember. He felt it to be educational when we were young and by the time that we were older our minds were pretty well made up as to what we believed and what we didn't believe.

How and when did he die?

He had heart trouble and he never went to a doctor unless it was really serious. If he said anything, Mother would say "Well, I'm sicker than you are." She just didn't believe he was as sick as he said he was. He died in 1967 and was 65 years old.

[William Clarence Radcliffe died in Ann Arbor, Michigan October 10, 1967 at the age of 70.]

Mother died in 1986. I think she was 86. She died ten days before Christmas.

Where is your father buried?

They are buried at Acacia Park in Bloomfield Hills. At one time it was Southfield, but now it's Bloomfield Hills.

What are the most important things you learned from your father?

I should have learned to keep my mouth shut, but I didn't do very well there. I learned a lot of mechanical things that girls don't normally know. I can do a lot of mechanical things that girls don't normally do as a result of watching my father and questioning him about things.

RJ Only was a very good friend of my father when he was young. Somewhere around World War One, RJ asked Daddy with four girls then he must have a favorite amongst the girls. He said "No, not really, but if I had to pick a favorite I guess it would have to be Virginia because she's the oldest. She was the first child and you're always more excited when the first child is born. But you don't love them any more than you do the other children." That hurt my feelings [giggles] because I had tried so hard to make up for the fact of him not having a son. I was a tomboy as a result. He never knew that.

What else do you remember about him?

Daddy?

Yes.

The thing that stands out in my mind is the fact that when he said he would do something, he did it. Oh, my back is bad. Also, it taught me not to marry a man that is a bully. Because the way Mother would get on to something and she'd stay to it until she got the answers that she wanted such as she was convinced that he had cheated on her. The fact is that he never did.

Would you be more comfortable if you sat in that chair in there and we did this?

No, not really.

How did your mother and father meet?

Through Mother's favorite brother, GL. In our first meeting I told you about that.

That was their first meeting?!

Yes. She had hoped he wouldn't recognize which sister it was. She hid her face so he wouldn't recognize anything else and I guess he knew.

So then I married Frank who was a bully, but I didn't know that because his personality didn't show at first. I saw what I wanted to see. I made a mistake [giggles first and then cries], but anyway, I have three wonderful sons.

Yes, you do. How long did your parents know each other before getting married?

About three years.

What do you know about their courtship and their wedding?

The fact that they had to get permission of the parents to marry, or you were supposed to anyway. I don't know whether Daddy ever asked his father or not. I really doubt it. He would have probably asked his mother, but she was dead and the father had remarried the twin sister. They liked each other. They admired each other so he talked to her. I'm sure he asked my mother's father permission to marry his daughter because that's the way you did things back then.

Clarence and Tella c 1923

Did they have a big wedding of did they have a small wedding?

They had a small wedding. They didn't have any money [giggles].

Was it just them and their witnesses or do you know if your mother's family came to the wedding?

No, I would say it was them and their witnesses because he was with the church at that point.

He came out of the army. When he was inducted, they had to stand in long lines outside in the pouring rain for physicals. That's how they did it. It just happened to be pouring rain so they had to stand there in the rain and of course it was all men. But still they had to strip and Daddy got pneumonia. They said he was dead and they sent him to the morgue. Somebody that worked in the morgue saw some flickering of some sort. I don't know exactly now what they saw, but they said "This man is still alive. Send him back to the hospital." They did and Daddy was saved.

Clarence Radcliffe during World War I

Prior to that he was kind of run down because he had had pneumonia as well as mumps that moved down. I think he had scarlet fever close to that time also. I remember him saying something about that. They told him he would never have children because of that. But he fooled them. That's what he always said.

Or your mother was fooling around!

Ah, that's where I came in...the adopted one [laughs].

Your dad joined the service after he met your mother?

He was drafted.

He was drafted after he met her? Before they got married he was already out of the service?

Yes.

What was their relationship like?

Daddy used to tease her a lot. He at one time was a great teaser. He'd put his arms around her and make her laugh. He made her laugh. When Priscilla came along, when I came along too, the family had grown to the point where it was work. So that it wasn't the family had grown past the bit where they had money to manage on, but the family kept getting bigger.

Does your family have any history of a particular illness, disease, genetic problems or addiction that could be passed on from generation to generation?

I don't know about the heart thing that Howard and Brian have. Howard says he was told that it was genetics. Daddy may have had that also, but we never knew it. The children wouldn't have known that anyway.

Does your family have any family myths or traditions?

Other than Christmas, Easter?

Did your family always do certain things on those holidays? The same thing every year that was important to you?

We made our Easter baskets. We made them out of paper, heavy paper. Heavy as we could find. We were shown how to do it and we were very proficient at it. As we got older we colored our eggs later on when we were old enough to know there was no Easter Bunny. Before then the Easter Bunny always colored them.

We always had our Christmas tree. Sometimes we didn't get it until they were all sold. Daddy got the last one on the lot. That was it. He would get it for twenty-five or fifty cents as a result of it not being sold. Otherwise, we wouldn't have had a tree during the depression.

Now we're just going to talk about you. Where and when were you born?

7/25/24 – July 25th 1924.

Where?

In Detroit on 24th Street. I was born in a hospital.

Was there anything unusual about your birth?

If there was I was never told, except that I had to have a copy of my birth certificate to get married. So we went down, had to go down there to pick it up and Mother had to go. We found out that I was listed as a boy. They figured that the lady who she was friends with next door had a son on the same day, practically the same hour that I was born. They got the birth certificates messed up. I was listed as a boy and her son was listed as a girl. The mothers had to straighten that out. Of course, I laughed about it. I said I'm supposed to be a son, I can prove I'm not. I can easily go in a back room somewhere and prove I'm a girl.

Do you know why you were given your name and does it have special meaning?

No, Mother said the doctor whose name was Bill, Doctor Bill, named me. She liked the name of Elizabeth, but she didn't know what to put with it. He suggested that it be Jean. So that's why I had Jean first.

If I hadn't gotten married, I probably would have gone all of my life without knowing that I was listed as a boy.

What was your birth order among your siblings?

Virginia was oldest. She was born on October 23rd 1919. Marion was born on March 26th. She's two years older than I am so she was born in 1922. Priscilla was born in 1929, I think.

She used to stink, that Priscilla, and I had to babysit her. Another thing that stands out in my mind – when she started school, when she got to second grade she wouldn't mind the teacher. They would call me in and reprimand her through me to tell her mother what she had done which was so wrong. Whenever I was called out of the room I knew what was coming up, that I had to go down and listen to a reprimand of Priscilla in front of all the children in her room too.

What stories have you been told about yourself as a baby?

That I weighed approximately, the doctor didn't have a scale, so he bounced me up and down in his hands and said "She's about ten pounds." And that's how much I supposedly weighed.

Do you have any other stories about when you were a baby?

No, but I have pictures of me with a bonnet on and so forth Somewhere one of the boys took a picture of me sitting in a chair with a yellow dress on. Does Howard have it? I don't know.

Elizabeth November 18, 1930

My hair was always dark. My eyes were so dark you couldn't tell the pupil from the iris. They looked the same. I always had bangs. They were cut straight. Virginia and Marion both had, Virginia to some degree, Marion some more, the same way with Priscilla, she had more curly hair. Then I came along with this black hair, straight as a poker. It was one of the many other things that made me think, whenever somebody said I must be adopted, that I must be.

Mother once told me, what a thing to tell a child, she said when she was lying in bed when she was pregnant with me, she was a superstitious woman, and a black man came up on the porch. She woke up and he was standing there looking in the window when she was pregnant. That's how I got my hair black. She was so frightened...Southern superstition. The black hair didn't last forever, a number of years, but not that long.

What are your earliest memories of your childhood?

Virginia and Marion were in school and other than having to look after Priscilla because I was the only one home with this baby. She was a very demanding child. They were in school and somewhere Mother had purchased, for I believe, two cents or something like that, the book of Shakespeare's Ivanhoe. Who wrote Ivanhoe? Was it Shakespeare? I had a hard time pronouncing the words and I didn't know what I was saying when I did. At least I knew how to sound them out even though I wasn't quite in school yet. I had broken my wrist. I was still home with that broken wrist with Priscilla. I was Mother's relief. All the sewing and all the work that goes with four children, four girls. Canning, canning all summer long to last through the winter. It must have been very, very difficult.

Sir Walter Scott wrote Ivanhoe. That's a pretty heady book for a little kid.

Yes, that's what I said. I could pretend. I could sound out words, but I didn't know what they meant.

When you were learning to read, did your sisters teach you since they were already in school?

If I asked what a word was, they would tell me how to sound it out. By the time I got to high school I just was an average, ordinary student, average. Marion and Virginia were all A's. I remember Mrs. Jones, she was a counselor. We were divided up by two counselors according to your last name and the R is for Radcliffe. It was Mrs. Jones who would check things. I was having a very, very difficult time with Latin and I asked to switch to Spanish. I remember her so well. "Well, your sisters can do it. Why can't you?" That's exactly what she said and that was about the tone of her voice. I had that all through school. "Your sisters can do it. Why can't you?" It made me feel stupid.

That was mean.

Yep. She could care less. She was putting in the time for her dollar. She must have been due for retirement pretty soon because she was totally white-haired and a little wiry. I can remember.

Do you consider your childhood happy? And why or why not?

Other than Priscilla, yes, I was happy because I had a good relationship with my two oldest sisters.

The youngest one was spoiled and even after I was married... I had my blouses, my clothes. The coat hangers were approximately four inches apart on the rod. They fit so tightly. That was just the way I had gotten to be. Priscilla would wear something after I had gone to work. She would go in my closet and pick something and hang it back up. She would never ask and hang it back up. She never said a thing. The next day if I planned to wear that blouse to work and found it was dirty and already used, that was the straw that broke, what do they say, the camel's back, or something? I moved out. I was so mad I moved out and went over and lived with Jones' for a couple of months before Frank got out of the service. Thanks to Priscilla. She always caused me trouble. Mother was very protective of Priscilla and I don't know why. She had always been.

Priscilla was always called Baby Doll until she went to school. They thought she was a cute little doll. She caused me so much trouble when she was young and until she was in high school that I don't have happy thoughts about Priscilla.

She had so much when she got married. Or course, she had to get married. But she had a big house. The only thing I can say about her is she fixed up that house like, like, [laughs] like it was a showroom. She loved Christmas and holidays. She decorated so professionally in her house. She ran up bills something terrible and Mother bailed her out. That's the excuse I have as far as Priscilla's concerned. She got so heavy. Geez.

She used to go down to the Fisher building where they had these exclusive, Hollywood exclusive dresses. Every now and then they would put these things on sale. She was like a size 44. She would buy something on sale because it was beautiful. It was one of a kind. She would try and lose weight to get down in it and of course she never did. All she did was run up bills and Mother bailed her out. It's too bad that she didn't pay for a psychiatrist for her instead, but back then psychiatry wasn't an accepted thing.

What were you like as child?

Full of fun and I was athletic. Always athletic and when I was in high school I was a majorette for Woody Herman. Do you remember Woody Herman? He was a high class, very famous big orchestra leader. That was his type of thing. He was into theater.

He was going to have a contest between all the majorettes in the state of Michigan. You had to be recommended just to be considered good enough to be in it. I remember I didn't have the costume. I bought blue slacks, a white blouse and white shoes, similar to tennis shoes, but they were shoes. The last two that were still on the stage after everybody tried out that hadn't been eliminated, that were still considered good enough to be against each other. Ralph Head was his name and he won first place for the state of Michigan as a drum major. He was very tall, thin and he was very fast. I had a good figure and I was very fast, but I didn't do any athletics that day because I had the spot light shining right in my eyes and I knew I'd never be able to see when to reach out to grab the bar as it was twirling. So I came in second in the state of Michigan. That was just one of my little athletic things. I was on the swimming team for a while, but it was a huge experiment.

I don't remember much of anything of Priscilla. I can't say anything about where there was any interaction between she and me. There wasn't anything exactly bad, but the way I felt, it was a bad association all through school.

She dropped out of school because she had to get married at sixteen. Then shortly after she was married she got money from her husband, Willard, and she disappeared. That time she went to Washington, D.C...no, Washington state. She was up there for a while until the money ran out and then she would call for help. Her husband would bail her out, but it got to the point where he wouldn't do it anymore and so Mother would bail her out to get her home because Mother was taking care of the babies. That's why she favored Willard because she practically raised him. I remember

Tell a when she was little, she still is, but she was very little in high school and she was on the team...what do they call them that does athletics and they throw them in the air before a football game?

A cheerleader?

Yes. She went out for that and being little she got it, of course, and she was always on top because she was so little and they could easily toss her. Well, they dropped her or she fell one day and she broke both arms. They took her home. They didn't take her to the doctor. They took her home. I think they tried to call Priscilla, but nobody was home. She said "Take me home and she should be home by the time I get there"...something like that. She was home for a bit before Priscilla got home. She was so frightened to tell Priscilla that she found her hiding in a basement closet. The basement was all finished off really nice and she found her hiding in the closet in the basement because she was afraid to tell her mother that she had fallen doing this. That tells you right there what the children's relationship was. They were afraid of her. She controlled them by yelling at them...frightening them. That was Priscilla. So we don't have to go to Priscilla anytime.

Describe the homes and neighborhoods in which you grew up.

We lived on St. Mary's...11635 St. Mary's in Detroit. It was a new home...new construction, a new home when we moved in there. It had no basement. I remember there was a wood stove in the dining room close to the kitchen door. We used to stand around there when we had been outside and came in from the cold. We'd stand around there to get warm around the wood stove. That was the first winter.

Men were going around during the depression and knocking on the doors and saying "Do you have any work that I can do for a meal?" It never occurred to them to steal. Daddy hired him for I don't know what, but what most people pay, this Indian fellow, after Daddy talked to him and realized that he had construction experience.

Daddy got all the books on how to do things and studied them. That summer he and the Indian raised the house and put a basement under the house and finished it...finished the basement. It was very nice. It had a large kitchen down there and we ate there in the summertime because it was so much cooler. On the one wall, I remember, were all these shelves and also they were lined with canned goods Mother had put up for the winter. There was a workshop and then there was a large room that we called the playroom. It had an old couch in there and it had a library table that Virginia's son Bill has today. Anything that Bill has like Daddy's desk, the roll top desk, Bill has and he took it all apart and finished it like brand new. He was the right person to give those things to.

The furnace was down there so there had to be pipes run through the house. The hot water system...I can't be sure now, but it seems to me that they put in a hot water system connected with the stove so all three floors were kept warm that way. The two of them worked all summer months from early spring on through to early fall. At least he had a job through the summer. I don't know what Daddy paid him, but he paid him as much as he could.

Every day Marion would, I remember her getting up on that library table. Daddy had made that table and it had shelves on each end. It was oak. Marion would get on there every single day if there was a baseball game, the Tigers. She was an avid Tiger fan and I can still see her sitting there with her legs crossed. She had created a score sheet and she kept track of what everybody did. The Tigers didn't have a better fan than Marion was.

There was a card table down there and we sat and did cards and stuff. When nobody was using the library table we would do our homework. Anyway, my childhood is gone.

Describe your family's economic conditions and other factors that affected your lifestyle.

[Laughs] Well, we rented when we first got to Detroit, on 24th Street. For a while Daddy did not have jobs, there for quite a while. That's when they worked on raising the house. That's when they did it all themselves, the Indian and my father.

I've forgotten how much it was worth, five thousand dollars. It seems to me it was around three thousand dollars they paid for that house when it was new. When they moved to Asbury Park I know they paid nine thousand for that house. They lived there until Mother died. She died there at that house. She loved that house. It was a nice house, very nice, three stories with a basement. My father finished it off. It was brand new. I have no idea...I know he never made a lot of money. He worked hard, but by today's standards he made very little. He made sixty-something a week that he made at that time. They had that house payment. Daddy was worried about that, I know. But Mother was determined and when boy, Mother was determined she worked hard and saved and managed. Other than that, that's about it.

Tell about your sisters and your relationships with each of them when you were little.

Well, we know Priscilla, don't we?

Marion, she was always very nice. The only time she wasn't, we were in the back yard playing. We were on a homemade teeter tooter. We were going up and down, Mother called for us to come in and we came in. That was always the thing with Mother. When she called us and we didn't do what she said, like come in, well then all we had to do is watch the kitchen door. If the shade was pulled on the kitchen door we knew we were in serious trouble. So that was the key, the shade on the kitchen door.

As a rule, I remember, going back a little bit. We just had the woodstove. It would have been the first year. No, it would have had to have been much later. I was about ten months old when we moved there to 11635 St. Mary's.

You were ten months old? Eleven, yes. I was walking. I was just walking. But my point is it was later than that time that this happened. It's a memory about Christmas during the depression.

We always got the same thing for Christmas during the depression. They saved very hard to get anything. Back when Daddy was lying in the hospital and I don't remember what we were talking about, but it got around to that and he said "I was always afraid that you didn't get enough at Christmas time because we couldn't afford anything at that time." We were happy and as a result I know I had every year during the depression I got a doll and we always had a new bathrobe. We'd get a bathrobe at the dime store, heavy flannel for ninety-eight cents or ninety-nine cents, something like that. The same way with house shoes because we got the doll, we got new bathrobes and the shoes and that's what we got for Christmas. We'd have candy canes, a couple of candy canes and that was our Christmas. We enjoyed it. We practiced for months to know which steps would squeak and which steps wouldn't squeak. The first one up had to wake the others so we could go down and make sure we wouldn't step on the squeaky steps.

Where was I? What was the question?

Your relationship with your siblings...how did Virginia and Marion treat you?

The only thing I can remember bad that Marion did was when we were on this teeter totter and she jumped off real quick. Mother called and she jumped off real quick and she laughed because I went down and hit the ground. She did it on purpose, so to speak. It was a child's way of fun. I remember looking at my arm and I knew it was wrong. It wasn't the pain that was bothering me, but the looks of it. It came to the wrist and then the hand dropped so the hand was lower than the arm. It broke all the major bones in my wrist and that's why I missed a year of school. They had it set wrong and they had to re-break it and do it over. That's the only thing that I did wrong or that she did wrong as a child.

The one thing I did that I remember is I could do cart-wheels and I was showing them how straight my legs were when I did a cart-wheel. I did it too close to Marion and I hit her face and I broke her nose. My foot hit her face and I felt bad because I didn't know. I didn't mean to do that. The same way she felt bad because she didn't mean to break my wrist either.

But other than that, I don't remember any relationship with Virginia except during high school. I remember when I thought she was feeling her oats, shall we say. She was getting dressed and she was in the bedroom. Marion was in there and Virginia was in there and Daddy knocked on the door. We thought she would say "I'm getting dressed. Don't come in." But she didn't. She told him to come in. Well, he did. But he was embarrassed because she had on underpants and a bra. Period. He was very embarrassed and he was terrified. I thought it was wrong and it was terrible. That's the only thing I remember about Virginia at that point. As adults, it's a different story.

> *Just prior to Thanksgiving in 2006 Elizabeth experienced a health problem that was life-changing. As a result she relocated from Arizona to California so she could be closer to Howard. She was a fiercely independent woman and insisted on living "alone". We were lucky enough to find a nice condo a few blocks from our home. This allowed her to live alone and yet have us near so that we could help when necessary.*
>
> *On the morning of August 2nd, I was up at 4:30 and heard an ambulance coming down the street where we lived. As it turned, I sensed a bit of fear that it might be going to Elizabeth's condo. I rationalized that it couldn't be as she always called us when there was a problem. About thirty minutes later, the phone rang and I recognized her cell*

phone number. A man identified himself as a paramedic and said he was on the way to the hospital with Jean Schenk and asked if I knew her. He said she had fallen out of bed and he was pretty certain that she had broken her hip.

After surgery she spent two months in a rehabilitation facility in San Diego. After three weeks at home "alone" again, it became clear that she needed additional help. Because she was so determined to continue to live "alone" we were forced to devise a way to get her to accept assistance. On October 18, 2010 Howard and I set out for Scottsdale, Arizona in our Lexus and a rented van. The van was loaded with things we knew would make Elizabeth comfortable for a two month stay in an "apartment" at an assisted living facility in Scottsdale. Among these things were her favorite recliner and her cat. Howard drove the van with the howling cat and I drove the Lexus with the howling mother-in-law. It was a trip I will never forget. Howard and I still argue about who got the worst of that one.

I was finally able to pick up where I left off with my interviews. They had become so interesting to me that I could hardly wait to start again. In transcribing the tapes we did after she got to Scottsdale, I noticed right away that there was a huge difference in her voice and energy level. Before the fall she had a difficult time concentrating and it was evident that her pain pills were getting the best of her. In assisted living, her medications were "regulated". She was eating regularly and well and she didn't have to take care of anything but her personal hygiene.

October 27, 2010

How did you meet your future spouse?

Which one?

Frank.

Oh. At school, we went to high school together. He showed me a great deal of attention and I was young and stupid and mistook attention for love. I hadn't developed enough emotionally to know the difference apparently.

Maybe he really did love you.

Maybe he did as much as he was capable.

Describe what your future spouse was like and tell something his background.

Is that John?

No, we're still talking about Frank.

Oh, okay. Well, he had the posture of a militant. He was a colonel in the ROTC which is the second highest position in the city you can be in the ROTC. I think that sort of went to his head. I don't know, but at any rate, that's the way it seemed to affect him. He was on the football team, although I don't think he was first string because I don't remember seeing him play very much.

If someone even looked sideways at me he would take off his glasses and turn and look at this person that looked at me and looked ferocious and say "Keep your eyes away from her. She's mine", was the way it affected him and those that were, I guess affected by it. Even when he was in the army, he was that way. If one of the army boys even looked sideways at me...when we were walking down the street in Louisville (I was living in Louisville for a short time) where he was stationed, I couldn't look at anyone, nor could anyone look at me without getting the' look', shall we say. He acted like he was ready to fight the war all by himself.

What did you know about his background?

Other than school, I had met his parents and they seemed to like me very much. In fact his dad wrote in a letter before we were married and I had it for a long time, but then I must have thrown it away or something or other. But his dad said that Frank was lucky to get me and that there weren't very many around like me so he should take good care of me. But I think the way it affected Frank was it was almost like getting a lecture and of course that didn't sit right.

Whatever Frank did, said, thought or you name it, he was...I swear, he was literally his mother's god. It made a person very uncomfortable. I know she told me that "You'll never take my son away from me." I told her I wasn't trying to, that I was just wanting to share him and that seemed to satisfy her a little bit. She would just as soon that he stayed in the realms of her desires and dreams and so forth. I had his father as a very warm friend, but his mother...I had to work at it.

That probably would have been anyone he married, don't you think?

Absolutely.

What was it about him that attracted you?

The fact that I guess I was young, hungry for love and I thought he was in love with me. Therefore, I thought I loved him in return. A teenage maturity is what it was.

What was your first date?

He had to borrow a car because he didn't have one so his dad lent him his. Another couple, his best friend and his girlfriend went along with us to the theater. That was our first date.

How did he propose?

He just said it. There was never actually a proposal. It sort of grew into the bit about well, we'll be married some day when he gets out of the army. I know his father bought the engagement ring, his mother and father. She encouraged him, I think because Frank didn't have any money so his dad bought the ring. I was working at Federal's and they brought it to me and presented the ring to me,

Who is "they"?

Frank's mother and dad.

Really, and Frank was away?

In the army.

That's Interesting.

Yes. After we were divorced Amy got married. I don't remember the timing, but I had it made into a little lavaliere of white gold because she's allergic to gold gold. Whether she still has it or not or what she's done with it, I don't know and I could care less. But I gave it to Amy.

What was your courtship like and how long did you know each other before you got married?

The courtship, he would come over to my mother's and my father's and we sat in the living room and watched television. He'd put his arm around me and we just sat there silently, but because of the silence Mother would come and say "Elizabeth, why don't you and Frank go downstairs to the recreation room and watch television down there?" That way she could keep an ear and an eye on things. If it got quiet downstairs, we got a call to come upstairs [giggles from both]. After a while he took the bus home.

[Not sure what they watched, but in 1943, it was probably not television.]

What was the other part of that?

How long did you know each other before you got married?

Well, about two years, I guess. But I was not emotionally raptured, shall we say, about him at the earlier point because I had my eye on somebody else. That was Al Plotz. He lost his sight because the retinas became detached in his eyes and they operated twice, but they couldn't do anything back then so that he became totally blind. So anyway, shall we say Frank was a last resort [laughs heartily]. Oh, dear! He would die if he heard me say that. That's the way it is. What's the next question?

What was the date of your wedding and tell about the ceremony, the place, the attire and the decorations.

I was married in black [laughs]. He came home on three days furlough. He had said "When I get a furlough, well then we're going to get married." Well he sent the time that we had, which was about two days ahead of time. Marion and I tried to find a dress. During the war it wasn't easy and so the only dress that fit me that was a nice dress, Marion paid for it, was a black dress. It was all lace across top and it was really a nice dress. We were married in the Methodist Church between Grand River and Schoolcraft.

On what date?

June 19th. I was going to say that I'm not sure of the year. But I have washed my mind of a lot of things from there.

Would it be forty-six? Did you get married the year before Howard was born?

No. I was almost twenty-three when Howard was born and I was nineteen when I was married. So it would have been about forty-four. I turned twenty shortly after...or forty-three. I think it was the beginning of forty-three.

You turned twenty right after you were married?

Uh huh.

You were married in June and you turned twenty in July and you were born in twenty-four so it would have been forty-four.

Forty-four. Well, that's the answer to that one, thanks to you.

You were nineteen and he was just nineteen?

Uh huh.

You were babies!

Yes, that's right.

You got married in a Methodist church. Were there decorations?

No, because we didn't have time for those things. There were no guests.

None?

None.

Your parents weren't even there?

Oh yes, my dad was best man. My mother was maid of honor. But they were the only ones that were there.

His parents weren't there?

Huh uh.

Where were they?

I don't remember the reason.

Okay, I can't stand it. How long did you keep the pretty black dress?

Oh, gee, I kept if for several years.

But you eventually got rid of it?

Uh-huh. I took it down to the Salvation Army.

Really?

Uh-huh. And when Howard was born Marion bought his baby carriage. I was just going to get a nice carriage, but of course I was gullible and wanted to make Mrs. Jones happy. She went along with me and she picked out the most expensive one there because she wasn't paying for it. Marion was paying for it. Back then I think it was eighty-four dollars which was a lot of money back then. I felt really ashamed to do it, but I was so gullible and so trying to make her happy that I did it. I never used it again after Howard. I gave it away.

Did you have a honeymoon?

In three days? His parents went and stayed one night with Aunt Bess. Aunt Bess was a good soul. She didn't have children, but she raised a couple that belonged to her brother. We had one day that we could do anything we wanted. We went out to Silver Lake and I had the worst sunburn that I've ever had in my life. I was one huge blister. It was terrible and then I think we just sat around and talked because I couldn't lie on my back. We sat around and talked for quite a while. On the third day he had to go back I think, to the service if I remember correctly.

At that time he was stationed where?

Louisville, Kentucky, I think I recall. That's where I went to stay for about a month or so. Then he was shipped someplace else and got his leg run over by a half-track and spent eleven months in the hospital. So that was our honeymoon.

What pet names did you have for each other?

None.

Tell about your first home together and what the community was like.

Our first home? Whether we'd rented or anything?

Your first home.

It was a bottom flat in Highland Park. Howard was five years old and Brian was a baby. If you ever had a child that caused no trouble, he didn't. He didn't even cry I don't think.

Brian?

Yes, he was a perfect baby.

Where did you live until Howard was five?

With the Jones'. Weren't we lucky? Frank was in school.

So you lived there?

Uh-huh, while Frank was in school. Then he got his degree and he went to work. I don't remember if it was the city or what, but it was for a water department. He tested water and things like that. He had an engineering degree. That was our first house.

What was the community like?

Well, it was old although well-kept. We lived there for close to a year with very little. The couch that we had was given to us by Mrs. Jones when she got a new one which was nice of her. There was a little store across the street that I used to shop at and I could walk to a Sears store when we lived there.

When Brian was just beginning to crawl, Mother took me out, with the kids, of course, to a wholesale place where they sold good carpets, but odd lots, sizes. She bought me my first piece of carpeting and I remember she paid fifty-five dollars for it. It was beautiful carpeting, very plush, very thick. It was a pale green. We still had pieces of it in the basement when we lived in Brighton. We used it down there.

Another thing Mother did for us...she bought me a washer, a Maytag washer. That cost her quite a little bit back then.

I remember when Brian was two days old. They didn't keep you in the hospital back then. You went home. I went home at the end of the first day after birthing. On the morning of the second day, I remember it very well because I was so uncomfortable. I had to go down to the basement and stoke coal in the furnace to keep the heat going all day long while Frank was gone to his job. I remember feeling that was something he should have gotten up a little earlier and done himself, but he wouldn't. You had to do those things or you suffered the consequences.

The neighborhood, it was nice people. There were some Greeks that lived there. I think more Greeks than anyone else that I can remember...a lot of Catholics. I used to cut hair for the neighbor's child and also the neighbor's husband [laughs]. I made a little bit, a very little bit.

After we were there for a little while with a new Maytag washer and a rug on the floor we moved. We bought a house and it was on Griggs in Detroit. It was a new house and it was nice. Two story with a basement, of course. There was quite a bit of new in that neighborhood. It was near Marygrove College.

Do you have a favorite story about being newlyweds?

The most outstanding story is the horrible blistering I got from the sunburn. When you were just married you couldn't participate in what is expected of young married people. That's the only thing that I can think of that was memorable.

Oh, yes, one other thing. Pa and Mrs. Jones went to Aunt Bess' as I mentioned. Mrs. Jones always starched her pillowcases. We all did back then. Hers had lace on it and this was an old set too. The next day she growled and fussed and so forth, saying that we had ripped her favorite antique pillowcase in our shenanigans [Liz laughs hysterically]. As I remembered that particular night we didn't do enough to rip anything [both laugh hysterically]. That's the only story I can remember about our wedding night.

November 4, 2010

What was your first year of marriage like?

My first year of marriage was interesting, I guess, because he came home on a three day pass and the first day I went out with Marion and bought a dress. We couldn't find anything on such short notice locally so we found this very lovely black dress. So I was married in black. It was basically an omen, I guess, maybe.

Frank was very attentive. He was very possessive. After a few months I went to live with him for about a month in Louisville, Kentucky where he was stationed. It was hot, but it was nice there. I could walk in to the market and shop. We had a very small apartment.

If another soldier or anybody looked at me, he would pull off his glasses the way he always did, probably still does, and turned around and gave him a killer look and say "She's mine and keep your eyes off" attitude. It was flattering to me. But of course later on I realized it was possessiveness.

I stayed in Louisville, Kentucky about a month and came back because he was shipped to Waco, Texas. That's where they were out on maneuvers after dark and there was no moon. He was running in front of the one front wheel of a half track, that's what it was called. The front of the vehicle has truck wheels and the back has wheels like tracks. It was dark and he tapped the hood of the side where he was running in the front, but the driver did not hear him. Frank stopped and the driver didn't and that's where one leg was crushed and he was in the hospital for eleven months. He wouldn't let me come down and see him. His dad went down there to see him, but he wouldn't let me come. I don't know why. He seemed to think people shouldn't see him unless he's in perfect condition, something of that sort, ego. But that was basically the first year.

After he got out of there he tried for, he worked very hard to get back in shape. He was asked or nominated, however it was, I don't remember, to go to OCS and that's where he became a Second Lieutenant.

[OCS was the acronym for "Officer Candidate School"]

How did you get along with your in-laws?

Well, I got along with Pa beautifully. Mrs. Jones, she was always very nice to me, but she was also reminding me constantly that this was her Frankie and I would never take Frankie away from her. Of course, she apparently examined the bedding. It was old, but very nice bedding, apparently, from what she said. She thought we had rough-housed and heck, all we did was go to bed that night, the wedding night. We were too tired for anything else. But she said it had a little tear in it someplace and we did it. She was nice to me as long as I let her be boss and always acted as if I was second choice and she was first choice.

Pa, he wrote me a letter that I threw away. I wish I hadn't. I threw it away about three or four years ago. In it he said, it was to Frank and he said, "You've got yourself a treasure of a wife. There aren't many like her. Take good care of her." That's the way he felt about me which was nice. It balanced out the other areas.

Howard says Pa was an alcoholic. I never once saw him drink at home like that. I never once saw him even anywhere near being drunk. So if he overindulged after they were divorced and he remarried, you know, maybe he had good reason to try and escape the situation.

Mrs. Jones called me up and she said "Do something for me" and of course I, like the little puppy dog fool went along with it. She said "I want you to…if Pa comes around with his new wife then you can make him welcome, but don't allow her in your house." But he never took advantage of that. He never brought her by. So I never saw her. I told her I would do that for her because I knew it'd be hell if I didn't [laughs]. But I didn't have to.

She was nice, like I said. She was very helpful as far as Howard was concerned. They both spoiled him rotten. I don't say this lightly. Frank was literally her god. She worshipped the ground he walked on and I'm sure that did a lot as far as the way he developed.

What was the hardest adjustment you had to make in that first year?

Being separated because the war was on and then Frank ended up in the hospital and I wasn't allowed to go down, as I said. Basically it was rather a turmoiled type of atmosphere.

When we became engaged, I'm backing up on something, I don't know whether I told you or not, I was working at the Federal Department Store in the men's shirt department and Pa and Mrs. Jones came by shortly before closing time. Pa had it, but she asked for it and she said "Frank asked us to get this for you" and it was the diamond engagement ring. But I know very well that Pa paid for it. Frank was making ninety dollars a month. How could he do something like that? That basically was the first year's adjustments.

What things did you argue about most in the early years?

We didn't argue because if he said something I jumped and his mother backed him up.

Well, that' the end of that question then. How did you and Frank resolve conflict?

I just answered it [laughs].

How important was religion in your marriage?

Well, at first Howard was baptized. He was the only one that was baptized and my father and mother came to the church as well as they stood up at our wedding, what wedding we had. My father held Howard during the baptism. He was the only one that was baptized. It was very important to me because I took the boys to church all the time.

Frank went with me to church when we were in Louisville, Kentucky. I'll never forget it because the one time he did, everybody was singing a religious song and it was one that they really poured their voices out rather loudly and he looked at me and he started singing that…oh dear, how did it go? [Starts to hum the tune to Vive L'Amour and then begins to sing the song.]

"Vive la, vive la, vive l'amour, vive la, vive la, vive l'amour, vive compagnie." That's it [sings again]. *"Viva la, viva la, viva l'amour."*

He was singing that out loud to the fullest with all the people around him singing a religious song [Liz bursts out laughing]. So I didn't ask him to go again.

So that answers my next question which is "Did you and Frank attend religious services together?"

Once. Twice, when Howard was baptized [Liz continues laughing].

Did you enjoy vacationing together?

The only time we vacationed together that I can remember at all was the day after we were married. We went out to Green Lake to some people that were good friends of my father and mother and the daughter was a good friend of mine. They let us stay there by ourselves for a day or so. I had the worst sunburn that I ever had in my life and I couldn't lie on my back for weeks it seemed like. That's a burn I'll never forget. I might have ended up having Howard sooner if I wasn't so burned.

What were the hardest times in your marriage?

Well, it started out...Pa was very secretive about how much he made and how much he gave to Mrs. Jones. That was the way he was raised and that was the way he dealt with the situation. He kept everything above and beyond what he gave her to buy groceries with. Well, Frank did the same thing. At first I got twenty-five dollars a week to buy groceries for Howard and Frank and myself. Then it went up to forty, I think it was. Then I finally talked him into going up to fifty-five dollars a week. Out of this I was paying utilities. We'd get behind and we'd get a notice that our gas was going to be turned off and he'd say "Don't worry about it. They know they're going to get paid." That was his whole attitude. "When I get around to it, I'll pay." He was working for the City then so that he was making I think it was a hundred twenty-five dollars a week. I remember when he first got the job, I thought "Good heavens, how can you spend that much money?" [Giggles] That was back in forty-six, forty-five.

Basically, I went to work for two reasons. One, to save my sanity when Katie started bouncing off my doors and banging and squawking and so forth and also to relieve the money situation that I had to deal with . You know yourself, he told you didn't he, that he controlled me by not giving me any money or something like that? He followed in his father's footsteps there. That was his teacher

You kind of have answered this. What was your economic status during your early years of marriage?

Yes, I'd say I answered it. I remember when I think I've told you so if I've done it on here stop me...about the baby carriage Marion bought. When Howard was born, Marion said she would buy me a baby carriage for a gift for Howard. We went to Sears...

You did tell me and you got the most expensive one.

Yes. Okay so I won't repeat that.

Did you move often during your marriage?

No. You mean before or after the service? Right after we were first married, I lived at home and I worked. Well, I got in a squabble with Priscilla because she was very lazy and she took advantage of people. Mother always backed her up for her bullish excuses.

I was very, very particular about how I ironed my blouses as an example. I never put a crease in the sleeves and in my closet my clothes were hung so far apart...my blouses and everything. It looked like a picture out of a magazine. I would go in there to wear something for work that I knew I'd put in there and I took it down off the hangar and looked at it and it was filthy. Priscilla would take my clothes and wear them and hang them back up and say nothing. That's when I got mad and Jackie Lou said "Well, come and live with us." Frank said the same thing and his mother said the same thing so I moved in with them... lived with them until Frank got out of the service. That was the turmoil. The move before Frank got out of the service other than the one at Louisville I told you about.

Afterwards we found a flat when he got that wonderful job with all that money...a hundred twenty-five dollars a week [laughs] testing water. I think that's what it was. We found a flat, an old flat. But it was clean and well cared for in Highland Park and we lived there until after Brian was born. Right after he was born we moved. We bought a house on Griggs and we lived there until Howard graduated from grade school. Then we moved to Northville. So I didn't move that much.

Why did you settle in Northville?

We found this house. You've seen it, haven't you? It was only twenty-three thousand dollars. They wanted to get rid of it so badly because they were in dire straits, the builder. They let us buy it with about, I don't remember exactly, but like a thousand dollars down. The very least, so they could get it off their hands and the bank gave us a mortgage so they got paid off. It's a beautiful area. The schools were good and Howard started high school there.

And finished there too, didn't he? Didn't all the boys go there?

Yes, all the boys did. 46930 South Chigwidden Drive.

She still remembers. What do you admire most about Frank?

He had beautiful curly wavy hair [laughs] once. He was a smart man. He never overly excelled in school, but he did well. In high school he was a colonel of the ROTC. There was only one higher position in the City of Detroit in the ROTC. He was on the football team in high school. He didn't play a great deal, but he was. Now do I admire it today or back then?

It just says "What do you admire most about your spouse?"

Oh, well [whistles]. Sometimes he would surprise me by being fairly nice. I can't really think of one definite thing.

What do you admire least about Frank?

His bullishness, his meanness toward people. That's only family, those that were closest to him. I've told you this before. In divorce court I told him "Frank, you'd enjoy life so much more if you'd just relax" because he was sitting like he had a poker up his back. He said "You, of all people, should know that I cannot relax unless I am in complete control of everything around me." That's his attitude and I admire that the least.

What have you learned about Frank over the years that you didn't know when you married him?

I didn't think he would run around the way he did. Katie wasn't the first. He never admitted it, but I know for a fact. In fact, my father had even seen him once. But he never said until just before he died. Huh!

It's just a complete circle of things that it's hard to pin one thing. His personality is just so complete, you know, he doesn't break away from it. Once he took me over to Cecil's house because they were going to practice skeet shooting and I hit them real good. So he actually relented and took me hunting, bird hunting with him a couple weeks later because he thought "Oh, she's good. She could get a bird." Well, I couldn't hit a thing because I couldn't kill anything. He got so mad at me because I wouldn't kill the birds. He never took me anyplace like that again.

[Cecil Lafond was Frank's best friend and perpetual hunting partner until Cecil died in 1978.]

How did your marriage end?

In divorce court [laughs hard] and very desperately. I'd rather not go into all of the stuff that brought it to an end because it doesn't do anything but hurt the boys to hear any more than they've been exposed to.

Do you care to tell how you coped with it?

I got a job and went to work; kept my mind busy.

How did it feel being single again?

Very good. It was like spring had flown. I remember coming out of that divorce court and the sun was shining and I felt I'd just had a fresh shower and put on brand new clothes.

What was different about your second marriage?

Oh, gee, everything. With John I had to be careful, I found out rather quickly. If I admired something in the store he would say "Well get it. You deserve it." Either that or a day or two later I would find it in my house. You know, he had so much confidence in me. Whereas Frank, he called once when we were working toward the divorce. I said "Well, I've come up with two propositions and you can have your choice. One is a hundred and fifty dollars a week for seven years. The other one is"...what was the other one? I don't remember now. It

Elizabeth with her second husband, John Schenk

seems to me like it was a hundred and twenty-five dollars a week for ten years or something. I don't remember, but anyway on the telephone he said "How did you come up with that? You're too stupid to think of it yourself" [so angry she was stuttering] and I hung up.

Is there anything else you would like to share about either one of your marriages?

Don't marry too early before you've developed and know what you need for a partner which is what I did...what a lot of people did

during the war. Who was it…somebody, my mother I think said that a woman is wise if she marries a man that loves her more than she loves him because she won't be hurt as easily and he won't give a darn.

When and why did you make the decision to have children?

Just the maternal instinct I guess and at that time I still felt I was in love with Frank and I thought maybe it would make him happy. I had two miscarriages in early stages in between Howard and Brian. With Brian I couldn't even ride in the car for I think seven months because it caused me to do things your body's not supposed to do at that point. But I think also it was a way of gaining something that was mine that I could love that would love me back. Frank didn't do it.

How many did you actually plan to have?

Two, I think.

What was your first pregnancy like?

Oh dear, I was living with Jones' and I remember to this day he said that he never did it and he did. I went to sit down to the table for dinner and he pulled the chair out from under me and I was eight months pregnant.

Who did that?

Howard, I mean Frank and I went to the floor and I broke my tailbone and that really hurt at birth when he was born. It was mean. Other than that they would say "Well you've got to eat for two. You've got to eat. Now you eat this. You've got to eat for two." I put on something like forty-five pounds that I had to lose afterwards. I think it was thirty-five pounds that I put on. Then I had to lose afterwards, which I did, but it wasn't fun either.

How, when and where did the birth occur?

It was forced because the military insurance, was it the military? I can't remember for sure, but we had hospitalization and it would cover the birth, Howard's birth, but it was going to expire in like two or three days. The doctor said I was already full-term which I was. He was the heaviest of the children I had, eight pounds something so they forced labor.

Where was he born?

He was born at Providence Hospital. My mother and father sat there all night because they started that in the afternoon. They came and they sat there all night and Frank did too, but he studied the whole time and slept. My mother was so annoyed with him because it was his first child and he was just reading. In her eyes he was reading and sleeping. Somebody came by and sat down with him and I remember him telling them or he asked Frank if it was his first child. He said "No, after you've had a few, it's all the same." That didn't make my mother feel very nice either.

How did your first child change your lifestyle and was being a parent what you expected?

Yes, as far as the parent as being what I expected. But changing my lifestyle it certainly did because it gave me, I mean to say, it gave Mrs. Jones something else to watch over and tell me how to do things and so forth and so on...criticize in a nice way. I told you what Frank said didn't I at the divorce? At least he gave me the credit for that. But he was gone all the time so he sure didn't raise them. He didn't even take them hunting with him, anything. No fishing, no nothing. That's really about all I can say to that.

[Frank actually did take Howard hunting from time to time, at least until Howard could figure out how to get out of it. Howard never shared Frank's enthusiasm for standing in ice cold water with near freezing temperatures and socks saturated with plant thorns and stickers waiting for the sun to come up so they could murder a deer.]

I always had a guilty conscience that I let Mrs. Jones push me into having Marion buy the most expensive buggy. It seems to me as I had thought of it that that buggy back then cost eighty-four dollars. That was a lot of money after World War II.

Give the names of all of your children, their birthdates and any circumstances that made their birth unusual.

Well, I will start by being critical myself. When Frank and I were in divorce court the judge asked him how old his sons were. He couldn't remember. I had to tell him.

So backing up, the oldest boy is Howard Alton Jones, after his grandpa Jones, whom I liked. I don't care what Howard says or anybody else. I liked him. The only thing he did wrong was the way he handled money with Mrs. Jones which is a big thing.

Elizabeth's three sons, (left to right): Jeff, Howard and Brian c 1957

The second son is Brian Clay Jones and I think I picked Brian as a name, but Frank picked Clay after Henry Clay Ford. And Jeff, I didn't want Jeffrey so we just named him Jeff, period. And his middle name, Francis, after his father. But I think he has the least respect for his father than any of the three boys do. I have discovered that since I've been out here which is interesting. All three are very good and they have their faults the same as we do as we're all human. But some people get a little overboard and forget what they're mad about.

When was Howard born?

Howard was born April 23, 1947.

And Brian?

Brian was born in 1954. No '52 It would have been...in 1952 on February the sixteenth.

My mother called me and told me to sit still all day and not move. She said no child should have to share a birthday with a brother or sister. So Jeff was born in '54 on February the nineteenth, three days after Brian's birthday.

You don't know why Frank picked Howard's name?

I think at that time it was partly Mrs. Jones. I would say really both of them. But I think she pushed harder than he did. He was hopeful to have a child named after him.

You mean Mr. Jones was hopeful to have a child named after him?

Yes, the father, the grandfather.

So that's where the Alton came from or was he Howard?

You know they found out later on when they got a birth certificate for him that his middle name was not Alton like he thought it was all of his life. It was Lincoln. Can you imagine the name of Howard Lincoln Jones? You know what that reminds you of? You know, well? You know.

No, I really don't know because it doesn't remind me of anything. Tell a story about each child's early years?

Early years, let's see, do you want me to start at the top or the bottom?

It doesn't matter to me. Whatever comes to mind.

Well, with Howard the thing that very often comes to my mind first was the time I was so petrified. It happened twice. Once he was just rolling over. He was just big enough to do that, so many months old. He walked at eight months, seven and a half month or eight months. Eight months, I think. Prudy walked at seven.

When I had that expensive carriage I used to walk into Highland Park because I was living in Highland Park, but I walked over there to Sears and just roamed the store daydreaming. It was a beautiful day and I would give the buggy a little push and let go of it. But I didn't see a bad bump in the sidewalk and the carriage turned over on top of Howard and I was petrified. I stood there and held him and cried like a baby myself. But he wasn't hurt at all. The blankets and stuff that were around him saved him.

The other time was when he, as I started to say, he just rolled over. I was getting dressed and I turned away from him for a second and he rolled over out of the bed onto the floor and landed on his head and I thought he'd broken his neck. That scared me to death. And of course, you know the criticisms I got from downstairs. We were living in the upstairs room at Jones' because Frank was in school yet.

Brian, now, of course, Howard would say I favored Brian. But there's no way I could, like I once told Howard, "What am I supposed to do, punish him for being good?" And it's true. When he was a tiny baby he didn't cry for no reason at all. If he cried you knew something was wrong and that wasn't very often. I used to call him either a sweet pickle or a sour pickle depending on if he messed his pants, his diaper, he was a sour pickle, but when he smiled at me he was a sweet pickle.

Jeff, Jeff had two older brothers. In fact, the thing I remember right away with him is Howard came home from school and came in to see the baby who had just come home from the hospital that day. I looked at him and he had chicken pox and they didn't even send him home and he came home exposing everyone including the newborn baby. Because I did not nurse, the baby got chicken pox, but it was in this order. Howard came home with it. He passed it to Brian. Brian got chicken pox. Brian ran in and looked at the baby before he came to see me and he passed it to Jeff. So they say the only way a baby does not get chicken pox is if they are breastfed and the mother has never had chicken pox. I never had it to my knowledge, I don't know.

You have to have had chicken pox because you had the shingles.

I know that, but I don't know when I got it so I must have been very small myself. But I didn't nurse my children because it was said not to back then. I had a problem anyway in that area. It was something I wouldn't put on tape. It was all ten days apart, ten, ten and ten.

I didn't get shingles, but Howard came home with mumps and guess who got them? My mother brought groceries over and she wouldn't come in because she'd never had them. She pecked on the dining room window and said "I brought some things over for you so you won't starve. I'll leave them on the back porch" which she did. I couldn't get out to the store to get anything and Frank didn't do those things. He ate on the road and it was up to me to provide for myself and the children.

Did you have any special pet names or nick names you used for your children and why were they chosen? You just told the sweet and sour pickle one on Brian. Do you have others?

No, I really can't think of any. I must have had something, but I can't remember. It didn't stand out in my mind.

Did your family move often and if so, how do you think it affected your children?

My family, you mean Frank? No, we lived in that flat until he graduated and got that job. When he got that job, his first job, testing water for the city or something like that, I think we were there for close to two years and then we bought that house near Meyers Road and Puritan. Well, you wouldn't know where that is anyway. But it was a nice area and I think we got it for ten thousand three hundred, something like that.

It was a two story house with a small kitchen. I know when I was pregnant for Jeff I reached up to the cupboards overhead

Elizabeth's first new home on Griggs in Detroit taken twenty-five years after selling the house

and my big fat tummy stuck out and caught my clothes on fire. But I got it right away so that I didn't get burned. But I could have been.

From there we didn't move again until Howard went to high school because of the school he would have had to go to. Because he was considered exceptional, they were going to send him on the streetcar or the bus down to Cass Tech in downtown Detroit where the exceptional student at that time was sent. That's were John went to school too.

Of course Frank or I either one didn't want a child that age riding on a bus and streetcar all by himself so we moved out to Northville. We got that house because the builder was going bankrupt

The house in Northville c 1971

and he wanted to get rid of it as fast as he could so it wouldn't go into the bankruptcy that he was going to go into. We got that house for twenty-three thousand three hundred, I think it was. Twenty-three seven, it might have been twenty three seven, twenty-three thousand.

In fact after I moved and it sold, the man told me when he took me through the house once, he said "I know exactly what you paid for this house because when we took the wall paper off the dining room walls they had written it on the wall with big numbers." The builder had done that.

From there, well we got divorced and I married John, but the divorce took two years and it sounds like we jumped from one thing to another and we didn't. I was alone there for more than two years, almost three. That's when I met John so we waited until Brian got married to Robin and then we got married.

Did you and John live in the house in Northville?

For a short time, uh huh and then we built, we were there just a year, about a year. He did a lot of nice things there too. I remember the time that, to give you an example of how well Frank took care of things. There was a leak, what caused it? It was upstairs in the bathroom and there was a leak and it didn't damage the walls up there, but it came down to I guess, the baseboard and it ruined the ceiling in the laundry room. Frank took something, I don't remember what and banged and tore out all of the wet stuff and it was a size about that big around (demonstrates with her hands) and it was like that for a good two years, at least before he finally sent somebody out to fix it. He never would fix anything because he said "Well, you're keeping a man from having a job. That's what he should do to hold a job." In other words," That's beneath me". That's the way he presented it.

From there with my second marriage, we built the house. John built the house out there at Brighton where I got my pilot license and everything. Although I got my pilot license in Ann Arbor, I did the solo work in Hyne Field in Brighton.

From there we moved up to...

Okay, wait, wait, don't tell me anymore about you and John yet because that's another chapter. I want to get back to your children first. Did you ever employ a nanny or guardian for your children?

With what?

[Laughing] That would be a no, huh? Okay!

You heard what Frank said, didn't you, how he kept control of me?

Yes. How did your family celebrate holidays?

You mean after we were married, or before?

You, Frank and the boys.

We always had a tree. The one Christmas that I really was hurt was they were all good except for this one time. He had been over to Katie's all day Christmas Eve and on the way home he stopped at the hardware store that always had a lot of good things for children. Well, they were sold out by Christmas Eve and he came home with a thing with little pots and seeds to grow herbs. Now would a young man, a young boy want something like that for Christmas? That's the type of thing he got.

The thing he got Howard that Christmas was, Howard remembers it, I'm sure, I know he does, was a radio controlled airplane, but he never would let Howard fly it. Another Christmas, he bought a nice gift. It was one of those pool tables that are so long, you know. It was a sturdy thing and it was good. That was supposed to be for Howard. Everything was always for Howard and was to be handed down if there was any handing down. But on Christmas Frank got Howard to play a game of pool with him, hockey, it was hockey, not pool. Of course, if it didn't go where he wanted it to, he broke the whole thing before Christmas day was over. He never replaced it and that didn't make Howard very happy. He felt, well you know how he would feel. But that was the type of…Another time he bought Howard the best Schwinn bicycle you could buy. That was the one that got hit by the car. So that's Christmas at our house.

We never got together with my parents. Frank wouldn't do it. He didn't like my mother because she would speak up. I remember one time particularly when Mother and Daddy came over. It was, I don't know, seven o'clock, something like that, maybe eight. Frank finally got home and he said "Why don't you stay awhile?" Well, they'd been there quite a while. He didn't come home and I was keeping my fingers crossed that the usual show didn't happen that night with Katie in the picture. Anyway, my mother made an excuse, she said no. It was a legitimate excuse that they had to stop and pick something up at a store before they got home and they would be closed and he turned to my mother with a sneer and he said "I wasn't talking to you Mrs. Radcliffe. I was talking to Mr. Radcliffe."

Describe a typical family activity or outing. This would be you and Frank and your boys.

Once in a century, it seems like [giggles]. But if we ever did anything it was on Sunday and we'd go for a ride in the car and then when we'd get home again he took off and we stayed home.

Maybe that's why Howard hates to take a drive in the car.

That's very possible.

Did you take your children on family vacations?

I did once because I, well yes, when his mother had her one kidney removed. We drove, we left Christmas day and we had to be in Phoenix by the next night. It was an awful snow storm.

Brian didn't want to go so we left him with my mother and my dad and he was happy about that. Howard got sicker than a dog on the way home. But it didn't show up until we went into a restaurant for breakfast and Frank asked him what he wanted. He said pancakes and eggs and it was a nice good breakfast. He ate it all. He was hungry. Then he went outside to go to the car and threw it all up. That made Frank madder than heck because he had paid for all that food and he threw it up. He was furious with Howard.

That was your only vacation?

Yes, that was the only time we went someplace as a family and Brian wasn't there. I took them to Florida once, just Brian and Jeff. Brian got the three day measles on the way there, came down with it. So I discovered that if you stay in air conditioning then the measles don't show the way they do if you know for three days. So that's what we did. I made sure that every place we went, every restaurant and every place we spent the night was air conditioned. Then we went on the Virginia's from there [both laughing].

Howard went to Virginia's after she had divorced Harry. He was another pickle, he and Frank. I don't know which one was the worst, but anyway we'll bypass him as to why I feel that way. I went down and stayed with Virginia when she was expecting Harry to come, young Harry. He doesn't go by that anymore. He hates his father very much. They all do.

He's not alive anymore, is he?

No, but he lived a long time with a woman that had quite a bit of money, hoping she'd die and he'd get it, I guess [laughs]. But he stole something from my father. My father invented, I can't explain it because I don't know enough about it. It had to do with a water softener and Harry took it, my father's idea and sold it to the company he was working for and said it was his idea. That hurt my father a lot. Anyway, what was the original question [laughing]?

Did you take your children on family vacations?

Well, I guess I answered that. I took Harry, young Harry, Cliff, he goes by his middle name, and Howard to Virginia's. I think I spent a week or ten days there. The other two stayed with my mother and when I got back I found out from the kids that Frank had taken the kids over to Katie's house and introduced them to her. That's when Priscilla was alive and she had young Willard there too. Virginia and I could never get over the fact that when she wanted young Willard to come over to her...she was fat then too and she would say "Here, Willard, here, Willard" just like she was talking to a dog. No kidding!

And he would come?

Yeah. I remember Tella, her mother wouldn't let her be cheerleader, but she went ahead and did it anyway. They wanted her because she was tiny, in ninth or tenth grade. I've forgotten which. They dropped her accidentally and it broke both her arms. She was afraid to tell her mother. When her mother came home she didn't know she was downstairs hiding in the closet because she was afraid to tell her mother. That tells you quite a bit right there.

But I'd have to say about Priscilla, Christmas and all the holidays, the birthdays for those kids she always went all out. She decorated the house. She made fancy dinners for them, for their friends and so forth. She really enjoyed that. She drew the attention to the one thing that she could do beautifully. Anyway, I get wandering off the subject. It's up to you to sort it out [laughs].

Describe a typical family mealtime.

For us?

Yes. This whole chapter is about you and Frank and the boys.

Well, if there was a family mealtime, it was with the two boys and myself, except on Thanksgiving and Christmas. He would come home late. He supposedly was working at the office always, always. He put on quite a little bit of weight on those holidays [laughing] because he ate two meals at Katie's house and our house. But he ended up losing it when we got divorced. But he gained quite a little bit of weight.

So he usually wasn't home for family dinners , not in the evening?

No. Never.

How about breakfast?

No. When we were first married, yes he ate breakfast with us...when we first lived alone by ourselves in Highland Park. But that didn't last very long. I can't ever remember him sitting at the table with the family on a regular day, being myself and the kids. But then they saw that he was gone so much when they were all in high school and they had different hours because of their different sports and stuff like that. So it ended up my having to cook different meals for different people because one didn't like that and one didn't like this. The pickiest eater to this day is Jeff.

Did you and your children attend religious services together?

Services? Regular Sunday services? No, by the time...well, I took Howard a number of times. But when we moved out of the Jones' then we didn't go anymore because Frank wouldn't go. It was too far for me to walk with the kids. Whereas when we lived with the Jones' we could walk it.

But you took Howard to church?

Yes, but he wouldn't remember it because he was real small.

So you never took them when they were older?

No.

Did your children have any medical emergencies or serious illnesses?

Let me think on that. I can't remember. It seems to me there was something, but I can't remember now. I'll have to tell you whenever I think of it.

What were your major concerns about your children as teenagers?

That they would get in with wrong crowds and lie to me about where they were going and what they were doing. But they, I'm sure they, you know, particularly Howard, fibbed a number of times. But he never did bad things except when his father caught him driving wrong. You've heard that story?

Yes, I have [laughing]. Well, I've heard his version.

He'd be the first to tell you that he was the only kid in the school on New Year's or whatever, at a party, he was the only one that his mother was out front to pick him up at eleven o'clock [both laugh].

He was probably glad if it involved dancing though.

Sure. It gave him an excuse if he wasn't very happy with the party.

Describe the personalities of each of your children and your relationship with them.

Well, they've always been good to me. Always. Howard used to test me periodically when he was in his teens. He would get mad and he'd say "I'm going to run away." And I would say "Okay, let's go upstairs and I'll help you pack." He'd sit on the steps going upstairs and he'd look pensive for a little bit and then he'd laugh and he'd say "I'm not going anywhere. I know a good thing when I've got it." That was Howard.

Brian, Brian was the kid...I swear if he did anything wrong it would shock me to death. Howard used to say "You never punish him. You never criticize him." I told him once or twice, "Well what do you want me to do, punish him for being good?" He was the kid that you didn't have to tell him to mow the lawn. And if you did, you expected him to do it good, but single mowing, but he never did. He would cross mow it in the hot sun in the summer. That's the difference between those two. Of course, Howard, I think he helped feed the fact that his eyes would swell up so that he didn't have to do these things.

Mother gave him a canary once. I don't know what ever happened to that bird. I don't think it died. He must have had to give it away because of Frank. I had to get rid of my favorite cat because of Frank. I kick myself ever since. I should have kicked him out instead. I told you about my cat, Miyoshi. I sent her by plane down to Virginia's daughter, she wanted it. That was the most beautiful Siamese cat I've ever seen. Ever...she was gorgeous.

What about Jeff?

Jeff, he...I don't know. I was afraid that he might get in the wrong...well, back up just a little bit. This tells you a little bit about the two youngest boys. Brian, there was a snow storm and they closed the schools early, but Jeff had forgotten his snow boots. So on the way home, and they had to walk a mile home, a little over a mile. They didn't call me. The school didn't call the parents or anything. They walked home. But Brian had his boots so he took off one boot and gave it to Jeff. They each had one boot that way.

Jeff, he... I remember when he was sixteen was when the marijuana became a kind of fancy thing to suggest maturity or something. He didn't smoke, but he came in smelling like marijuana once and he started to cry. I'll never forget that. He put his arms around me and he said "Mom, you should know that I wouldn't do those things. The other kids would, but I wasn't. I would never do anything to hurt you". That's what he told me. And to this day, he's very warm toward me...very warm. But of course, with this thing between Howard and Jeff...it's sad really, because well, at one time Howard and Jeff were like this [holds her index and middle finger together] and they wouldn't have anything to do with Brian. Anyway that's my story and I stick with it.

So what is your relationship with each of the boys?

Well, I trusted them and yet every once in a while I would double check to make sure that my trust was not being misused. And I never found that it was.

But even now, what's your relationship with them?

Well, you know Howard. He can be pretty darned... he can be pretty brutal when he gets mad and yet they don't come any better than he is. Look what all he's done for me. And Brian's the same way. Jeff, he's very warm toward me, but he's over there in left field somewhere. He doesn't know what he's mad about. But anyway...

November 10, 2010

Can you share some memorable moments about each child's teen years?

Teen years...well, with Howard I could probably come up with more than one. One was the fact, you've heard, where he was driving and he zoomed past a car on the wrong side and sped around him and it turned out to be his father. That's one. And another one was when he and Dave...what was Dave's last name? Howard would know. Dave, Dave, Dave, Dave. He's a doctor now. Anyway, they went swimming in the lake over by the graveyard that's on the hill. There's a good, nice little lake over there, nice clean water and et cetera. And they dove in and they were swimming and having a great time when they saw a casket was coming out of the earth where it had worked its way out due to rain on the soil getting wet. They reported it to the city because it had to be retrieved and redone.

Dave Kerr.

That's right, you're right and you didn't even know him.

No, I didn't, but Howard talks about him.

And of course, I remember how he was the star of the football team. I went to all of the games but Frank never did. His son was the star yet Katie was more important. But Howard adjusted well. He knew what was going on far more than I realized he did. He had a phone in his bedroom, which he had begged to have for some time until we relented. Every time it rang, I turned it low, but still it rang pretty loud. You know, twelve o'clock, one o'clock in the morning when it rings it always sounds several times louder than it really does normally. I got so I buried it in the pillows, just literally buried it in the pillows in the other bed because it wasn't just her. Her husband was calling. He'd get drunk and he would call and swear you know, when the phone was answered. He'd swear into Howard's ear because Howard sounded like his dad on the telephone at that time and threatened him and all sorts of things. I remember one night when Howard came home about two o'clock in the morning and he said that her brother...he had roamed around because her brother was after him and threatened to kill him.

[Howard has no recollection of this ever occurring and didn't even know she had a brother. However, if Howard was coming home at two in the morning, his memory may not have been in tip-top shape or more than likely, the "brother" seemed to be a good excuse for a rather tardy arrival.]

After Howard?

Uh huh.

Katie's brother or somebody ... [Elizabeth nods] Oh, really?

Uh huh and he went down stairs and laid on the couch and went to sleep just like that. I didn't understand how he could do that so it made me wonder if the whole story was made up. You know, he told me quite a few interesting stories through the years there [laughs]. That's enough of that. There was such involvement in his life there that it has to be a part of it. When I think about his years then and so that...

Brian... Brian was on the school wrestling team. And the state trials were over, the state the contest I should say, not trials, were over at some high school way out someplace. I don't remember where now, but it was about fifty miles west of Northville and he wasn't going to be wrestling until I think it was eleven or eleven thirty that night because the different things took a lot of time. I drove over there and drove back afterwards and he came in second in the state. The referee, not the one that refereed his match, but the one that was watching, came over to him afterwards and told him that he should have won, it was a bad call and he should have won that match and got the gold medal. As it was, he got a little silver thing that was only silver on the outside and it wore away.

I remember the time when we lived on Griggs he wanted to make some money so he went around to the different neighbors and I think he was asking fifty cents to mow their front and back lawns.

This was Brian?

Uh huh. I can't think of the lady's name… Schwartz or something like that, I think it was Schwartz. I was talking to her a few days later after he had done her lawn, but when he came home that day he had told me how she had tried to talk him down from fifty cents to twenty five cents to do the front and the back yard. I was talking to her a few days later and she said "Oh, he did a very good job." I said "Yes, he told me that you had tried to Jew him down" and after I said it I realized she was Jewish. She said "That's alright. I've heard that before." But she was good about it. But it just popped out of my mouth before I could think [laughing].

He and Jeff both had their tonsils out the same day and of course you know that. Howard corrected me.

Howard said he had his tonsils out too.

Yes, but not that day, another day, a year or two earlier. Maybe three years, I don't remember that one. I remember Jeff cried and Brian tried to console him by telling him to think about the ice cream he was going to get. Their beds were side-by-side.

Jeff… the only thing I can remember that was really unusual, we're talking about Jeff, was the fact that the school had a big trophy because they had been champion in their league and they had a big trophy this one year and before any of my children were there. They kept it in a glass enclosed cage in one hall. Nobody had ever been able to steal it and get it although it became an obsession for people. Well, to this day Jeff never told how he did it, but Jeff and another kid stole it. They closed the cage back up and nobody knew he was in it except the trophy was gone. I don't think they ever found out that he did it, that he was the instigator. He was very proud of course, but he didn't dare let them know.

Which child is most like you and which is most like Frank and how?

Let's back up a little bit. You knew that all three kids had a Volkswagen. Frank wasn't around to do it. Howard had a, I don't remember the color of Howard's. It was like a red, probably red and Brian got a blue one, I think and Jeff got an orange one. It may have been the other way around. Yes, I think one was yellow and one was orange. I remember that aggravated Frank so much because he thought it was belittling to him. He said the least they could have gotten was a GM product. I said "Well, really, it's what they wanted and they paid for it."

The only car Frank ever bought the kids was Howard's and he bought that Triumph. It had six cylinders and when one cylinder went you had to send to England to get a replacement. Then you had to buy a full set because they didn't sell them individually and that made Frank go through the ceiling. That's the end of the kid's stories, finally. Let's see, where were we?

[The car was actually a 1961 MG-A with a four-cylinder engine.]

You were going to tell me which child was more like you and which child was more like Frank and why?

I would say Howard was more like Frank because he was testy. He still is to a degree. But I wouldn't tell him that at this point. Although I did once when I first moved in with you, sometime when I was with you and he didn't like it one teeny weeny bit. But he was being bossy and so that I thought that "Well, he didn't get that from me."

Everyone has always said that Jeff looked like my dad. As far as Brian is concerned, everybody has always said that he looked like me. I think he has always had a temperament that I have. When I was younger even I would give in and try to bring harmony into a situation.

Did any of your children have any exceptional talents?

Oh yes, they all did, really.

Well, there's a mother for you [laughing]! Okay, what were they?

Well, Howard, his talent has been learning another language, music. If he had had a decent teacher to go to when he was younger, I think he would have been a really good pianist. There for some time he really could press out a good ragtime, something of that sort.

Brian...he had a teacher that was good, but shortly after he went to her...she was very impressed with Brian. She said he really had a natural talent and he should keep it up. This was in Northville and shortly after they moved away. I don't think he had more than four or five lessons and they moved away so the good teacher was gone. There was one other teacher there and that was the one that Howard had and she would discourage anybody. She was an old fuddy duddy that I don't know who you could compare her to as far as teaching was concerned. It certainly didn't encourage anyone to be good at anything.

Howard, of course, excelled in sports and Brian excelled in sports. His was wrestling because he couldn't compete, he wouldn't compete with Howard on any other sport because of the competitiveness. Back then Howard and Jeff were very close and they sort of pushed Brian away because Brian didn't get into trouble, you know, just petty trouble that kids are known to do. But the others did and they didn't see it that way at all. Jeff had a good sense of humor. Howard, I swear, don't tell Howard this, I don't want Howard to read it, but he used to enjoy actually encouraging Jeff to do things against Brian.

You mean when they were kids or later?

Yes when they were kids. I used to feel sorry for Brian because of that. You know, he didn't do anything wrong and they resented it. Howard particularly resented it. Maybe Jeff did too, I don't know, but he never said it, whereas Howard spoke his mind.

I remember once when Jeff came home after being out with some boys and girls and he smelled of marijuana, but not his breath. But I still asked him "Well, then how come you have the crumbs of this in your pocket?" And he said "Well, the kids put it there for a joke" and I thought "Oh, yeah, there's another phony." But he started to cry and he put his arms around me and he said "Mom, I would never do anything that would hurt you." I'll never forget that because he was really sincere. There wasn't an ounce of fibbing or making up a story in him at that point. If he did something and you asked him, he would admit to it. But like anybody, if you're accused of something and you didn't do it, you really get verbally nasty about it or else you did what he did which was hurt him badly. I hurt him badly by accusing him. That's when he put his arms around me and told me that he would never do it. He loves me and that he would never do anything that I wouldn't like and that would hurt me.

But he's doing it now, isn't he [both laugh]? But I've often wondered if they all got back together again, all three of them... I think I should have had two or four kids of the same sex because with three it's always two picking on number three. I think that it is in boys anyway. I don't know about girls. I was ostracized to a degree by Virginia and Marion at one time. Virginia was the instigator when we were young. Priscilla was almost six years younger than I so she was just naturally out of it due to age and underdevelopment and growth...mental growth and physical growth. But I often wondered if they got back together now all three of them if that pattern would surface again. Instead of three being warm toward each other two would have a tendency to ridicule the third.

I think you grow out of that, don't you think?

Well, I used to think so, but it proved not to be so in my family...in my boys. Yet, look at your family, but you're girls so I don't know.

Howard is not like his father anymore. I really see a difference in him, I really do. I see a difference in him and writing that book _The Man on the Bench_. It's almost like he's looking at situations and everything from a softer point of view. I don't know. But he sure is...I can't complain about him now. Only once since I've been living out here has he ever been sharp with me. That's when we were going into a restaurant over near the hospital somewhere. I don't remember what brought it about now, but he raised his voice to me. It was the hint of the old Howard.

Describe your parenting style including discipline. And did it change over the years? And how did it compare to your parents style of parenting?

Two different generations, just like any other generation situation in my age bracket. You know, they were brought up in families where they didn't show emotion, they didn't show love, they didn't show pride very much. My mother never told me she loved me 'til just before she died [crying].

Even when you were a little kid?

She put her arms around me once. I remember that [openly sobbing]. I had been falsely accused of pushing a little kid off the porch and anyway, the child cried. She had fallen off the porch herself. I wasn't even by her, but the father said that I must have done it. He was inside doing something. He wasn't even there to see what happened. I remember Mother got very mad about that. She went over and she told him what she thought and what really happened. She was sewing that night and I had been crying ever since that happened and because she put her arms around me and I liked it so much that I didn't want it to stop [laughing and crying]. So I sat on the floor next to her and I laid my head on her lap and I kept crying and trying hard to cry. I remember that so well and I got to the point where I just couldn't bring up another tear. Even at that she didn't say anything to me. She patted me once when she put her arms around me. She wasn't a demonstrative person at all, not in the least. My father really wasn't much either in that area. They didn't do it then.

Were you demonstrative you with your children?

Yes, but not as much as I think I should have. Yes, because they were boys and I felt that I didn't want to sissify them, not having had a brother and what have you. I was young and trying experiments. I always felt sorry for a first child regardless because they're experimental children.

Did your parenting style change over the years?

After I married… not Frank, after I married John. Frank…he was never demonstrative, but John, of course, was. He in a way taught me to feel a response in giving a person a hug and getting a hug. Does that make sense to you?

Yes.

I'm maybe more so than I should be now. I don't know.

No, no, I don't think anybody can hug too much. Did you and Frank have any major differences about how to raise your children?

No, he wasn't around very much. He was either golfing or out playing ball or something or gone with Katie depending on what time of the marriage it existed. Anyway...oh well, you learn from all the experiences.

You were a step-parent, but not when John's children were little, but were there difficult aspects of being a step-parent?

I was afraid there would be at first, but there wasn't because I told them that I wasn't trying to replace their mother. No one could ever replace your mother, but I did hope to be there for them. That's what I operated on. But now, you know, Debbie tells me she loves me. She said when I moved away she felt like a part of her body moved away too. She's a good girl and I tell her I love her once in a while because I admire her greatly.

Have your parents played an important role in the lives of your children?

With Brian and Jeff. I remember the time I had gotten a little black cat. It wasn't a year old and I had just had it spayed and we were at Mrs. Jones'. I guess I told you this. Mrs. Jones was always calling me at work just to say "How are things going?" No reason at all, really and they didn't like personal calls at work. I told her that, but it didn't affect her. She was more important or thought she was. This one day... Jeff loved that little cat. Brian did too, but Jeff really loved that cat. I came home from work...I got home about quarter to six, something like that and there she was standing at the door and there stood Jeff beside her holding a dead cat.

This was your mother?

No, Mrs. Jones. He was holding a dead cat... his cat. She said "Oh, Frank ran over him accidentally, but he ran over and got in a bush there so I thought he was okay." She never mentioned that in the four or five times she had called me at work. I would have gotten off work and taken it to a vet and at least had it put to sleep or something. But that poor little kitty had suffered for hours and Jeff cried, oh how he cried [crying]. I took my best throw rug, it was one of those rugs... it was a white throw rug about oh, that long, about that wide [holds up her hands to demonstrate]. It was furry and fuzzy on both sides. You've seen that kind. I wrapped the kitty in that. Jeff and I went and found a place where we didn't think it would ever be disturbed and we buried it [crying hard]. I'm getting soppy.

That's okay. What kind of a role did your parents play in the lives of your children?

Daddy played more in Howard's. He liked Brian a lot, but Jeff wasn't around him, hardly much. Brian stayed with them for the week that we drove out here (Arizona) after Mrs. Jones had her kidney removal. I need a Kleenex, please. She had a kidney removed and on Christmas day we drove out here and Brian didn't want to go. Mother said "Well, we'll take him" and she did

Mother always loved children, always did. She always said that there's something pretty about every child. You focus on that one thing and compliment the child on it. If it has beautiful eyes or if it has nice hair you tell them what lovely hair they have or what pretty something or other they have. You always compliment them, brag a little bit to them about how they looked or what have you, how well they did or something. But she mellowed and changed through the years too, to a degree when it came to children because she practically had to raise Priscilla's. As Priscilla would save enough money she would go to the bank and take it out of her account and disappear. She didn't tell anybody where she was going or that she was going. She finally would call when she ran out of money and my mother would always send her money to come home. She was married. When I say come home, it was to her children. That's why Mother, I think, favored young Willard so much. He might just as well have been her child because of all the care she had to give him. But we learn from all experiences, good or bad.

What is the proudest moment you had as a parent?

Proudest? [Laughing] The first thing that popped into my mind was I was working in the credit department at that time at Consumer's. I hadn't been working very long there when Howard was taken...he belonged to the... applied to be taken into the Thespian's and the auditorium was full of parents and people. Their kids had tried to get in. They had to write their speeches and all that stuff, if I remember correctly. When Howard gave his speech, the people behind me, right behind me, said "Who is that boy? He's wonderful". Of course, I turned around and I said "That's my son, Howard Jones". [Laughing] I never did that before in my life and I haven't done it since. But anyway, the next day I went to work, I'm sure I've told you this story, and I went to work and after I got in there and sat down at my desk and I said it loud enough for everybody in the room, which was double the size of this place here, might be bigger than that, about three or four times this size. Anyway, so I said it loud enough so everybody could hear. I said "I'm so proud of my son. Last night he gave a speech and he was taken into the Lesbians." Your mind says one thing and your mouth says another [laughing]. Have you ever done that?

Oh, yes [laughing].

I'll never forget that embarrassment. But of course, it was pride.

What is worst part of being a parent?

Changing dirty diapers [both laughing].

What is the best part of being a parent?

We didn't have store-bought diapers back then, you know. The best part? The love a baby, or a young person shows you and you show them back.

What was it like for you when your children left home?

They were all adults when they...they really weren't, it was after the summer vacation and the time between high school and starting college. I think if every parent is honest they enjoy the quiet, but also they feel like they've lost something too. But you adjust very quickly. I think women adjust to situations, all situations far better than a man does and I think that's why our genetic makeup has us live longer as a rule than a man.

Is there anything else you would like to share about parenthood?

Teach a child to know discipline, know what it is to properly apply it to their lives. To never give a child everything they want, never. Let them earn it if they want it badly enough. They appreciate it much more.

November 17, 2010

Describe the area, city, small town, farm where you spent most of your teen years.

City... at my mother and dad's house which was in the city of Detroit, but in the extreme outskirts. It would be sort of like...you know where Livonia is?

Yes.

It would be sort of like...out in the country, but Livonia was...nobody around at one time. That's the way it was with our house. It was out...it was a new development.

Describe yourself as a teenager. What things were important to you?

Being cared about, to be outstanding and to get my mother and particularly, my father's approval. It was very important to me because my dad didn't have a son and I heard him say all men want a son. So I tried very hard to be a tomboy so that I would be a substitute for what he was missing which was a son, of course. But even as he laid...he died in the morning around noon, if I remember...Howard will tell you that. He was the only one that was there. But I was there the night before up until about eleven o'clock at night and we talked and talked and talked, Daddy and I did. I remember that, him watching me.

William Clarence Radcliffe c 1929

But anyway...

I was an awkward kid in grade school. When I got to high school I started to blossom. I went out for... I was a good tennis player. In fact, I signed up for tennis as a gym project. Everybody had to play a round if they could with the teacher, Mrs. McGowen, to see where they stood in their ability. In other words, you didn't play a game you just played a round, so to speak and I beat her. And she said "Well, you'll get full credit for this course, but you won't have to take it." So then I was put into a higher tennis program there. But my big interest although I liked tennis, I used to go over there and bounce balls off the side of the school and to hit back and so forth. But my big interest was diving and swimming. I didn't make the swimming team, but I did make the diving team and of course I lost the ability for that a long time ago.

How old were you when you heard your dad make that statement about "Every man needs a son"?

I was about seven, something like that, seven or eight. Every man wants a son, not needs.

Did you think he didn't approve of you?

Oh, I know he did because he took me in the dead of winter, he would take me on his electrical jobs. In fact, Ralph Boles, I helped Daddy when he wired Ralph's house. I'll never forget it because Daddy's hands from the cold...you can't wear gloves and do electrical work and his fingers were all just split practically to the bone and bleeding from the cold. It was terrible. But I saved him a lot of steps and that was basically my job. I felt that I could do something to help him anyway. I used to go alone and enjoyed it because I could talk with him far more easily than I could talk to my mother, always could. But I didn't say enough after I was married. I wish I had.

What do you mean?

Well, Mother accused him of cheating on her which he never did, but he got tired of Mother. When she got an idea she was like a bull dog with a bone in its teeth. You don't just get it away from them and she hounded him with that. She was positive that he had cheated on her when he went out on a job or something. I'm telling you it broke my heart. One day he came over to our house on Griggs. I'll never forget the scene because he sat in the chair and he was so tired. He looked like he hadn't slept in days and he said "Your mother's at it again. I never cheated on her on my life and at this point, I certainly wouldn't anyway." But he was tired of being accused of something he never did, you know. She hounded him in that respect.

At one point when he had his first heart attack, in the hospital she was hounding him when Marion was there. Marion had come from California. When Mother was hounding him and to shut her up he said something like "Well, I did it" or something like that just to shut her up. Marion always said "Well, it had to be true or he wouldn't have done that." I told Marion why he did it, just to hush Mother up. Marion didn't want to believe it because she was all Mother, all Mother. That's perfectly all right, but not when in my mind it was so obvious the strings she tested them and what she did with them.

I didn't mean to interrupt you about what was important to you when you were a teenager and you talked about being on the diving team.

Yes, and then I branched off to when I was married and Daddy came over because he knew that I believed him. He just needed reassurance. That's sad. But anyway, who's the card for?

That's your card. It's your Mother's Day card that you keep in this book.

Oh, yes. I ask that every time, don't I? What's the next question? Oh, I know, back to the teenage years.

I was the best drum majorette they had. In fact, I eventually won the city championship and the Michigan championship for girls. Ralph Head won for the boys. That was with Goodman...Benny Goodman. He was a well-known band leader. My impression of him was all the makeup...I never realized how much makeup they put on...thick. It was amazing. I don't think they do that to the degree they did then now. I don't know.

But anyway, Mr. Hargraves the head of music, the head of the orchestra and band and the small ensembles, he told me to come in at four o'clock, that he wanted to correct something I was doing wrong in marching. I thought "Oh, dear, I'd better go." So I went. He had me march toward him. "Raise those knees high, higher. You want to keep those knees high when you're marching in the front." Then he had me turn and walk away to see how I picked my feet up in the back too. One time as I walked over to him, I'm sure I've told you, he took hold of my hips. The first thing I knew his hand was between my legs. But of course back then, we didn't have money for Kotex and it was fairly new on the market. It was one of those special things. We used old rags so that they were thicker than the average Kotex and he got a handful of old rags. I think he was sorry he did it [laughs] and I certainly turned against him. I never again would see him by myself, ever. Then I found out that he did the same thing with Jackie Newell only her name is Jackie Chambers now. She married a fellow we went to school with.

That ring is pretty on your finger with your ring. It really matches, you know...looks like it was an original set. Funny, I can appreciate it more on your hand and what I gave Deb and so forth, because of your youthful hands and nice personalities and they all reflect in the total picture. I really enjoy it more than if I had it on my own hands. I enjoy the jewelry more.

I think it's very nice.

I'm so glad since you got it. You'll wear your good one for special occasions.

This is a good one.

Well, yes, that's a good one, but not to the degree that the other one is. It cost larger zeros.

I think nice jewelry should be worn every day.

I agree unless it's going to damage the jewelry.

What do you remember most about your school experiences while a teenager?

I remember being impressed with one boy, Al Matheny, He didn't know I existed, but I thought he was awfully nice. When we had the fifty year reunion I went to it because I was in the area at that time visiting Mother. It was right after I moved up north. Or was it up north or to Brighton? I've forgotten which. It was up north. He was there with his wife and I told him, I laughingly told him "You didn't know that I had quite a crush on you in high school." I made fun of the whole thing and he did too. It was a lot of fun that night. We had a lot of jokes between a lot of people who were afraid to even speak to them when we were younger. Yet we had gotten older also and more mature. With age you can say things that you couldn't say otherwise. I find that with old age also that you can say things you wouldn't be able to say and have it taken the proper way if you were younger.

I told you how I went to stay the one summer with Margaret and Max. Max, Margaret's husband he taught me what a French kiss was by doing it.

Daddy's father, he said "Well, give me a hug." So I gave him what I thought was a regular...a child...I was thirteen...a hug to their grandparent and he went down to my buttocks and pushed my buttocks into him so that I would feel that there was something there. I'm telling you I came from an oversexed background. I never told Daddy that and I never told Mother because Daddy hated his father for other reasons [laughs]. He just started talking to him just a very few years before he died. That sounded like the telephone.

It's your cat meowing.

Is that you? Well. I remember the time I was thirteen, fourteen. How old was I? I was in high school so I had to have been at least fourteen. I was more like sixteen, I guess. Mother had me out in the backyard on this hot summer day weeding around her roses. I've got a picture somewhere or I had one where I look like the most awkward kid on the face of the earth. No personality is what it looked like in that picture.

Always an animal lover, Elizabeth rests with her cat and two dogs.

Ralph Boles and his mother came over because he had just gotten out of the service and he had his uniform on and he said "I heard you got married." He had talked to Mother first. Yes, so I had to have been nineteen anyway because I got married at nineteen. He said "I heard you got married while I was gone." I didn't say a word and he said "What'd you go and do that for" in just that tone of voice and then he turned and walked in the house [laughs]. Personality plus, also.

I made my grade school dress for graduation and I made my high school dress for graduation. The grade school dress was maroon. Was it maroon? Polyester was just coming out. It felt like silk, but it wasn't. It was polyester. It was maroon with white flowers. I don't think I have a picture of that.

Marion was still in high school when I started at Cooley. To follow a sister that makes all A's, two sisters, is no fun. We had a counselor there, her name was Mrs. Jones. It couldn't have been something else. It had to be Mrs. Jones. She would say "Well, your sisters do it. Why can't you?" And I felt like walking out. I wished I had gone to Redford. We had a choice. We were right on the line so we could have gone to either high school and I wished I had gone to Redford, but I didn't. It was a little farther. I thought it

Elizabeth in her hand made graduation dress in 1943

would be fun to have sisters that were so smart, you know. I would be looked up to rather than ridiculed because I would be called the same thing. But that's the way it was.

Were you involved in extra-curricular activities in high school?

Yes, in the respect that I was on the swimming team for one year. I was in the choir and I was of course in the chorus also. I was in the orchestra and I was the drum majorette for football games in the big stadium downtown. So that got me the attention I needed. But I got the wrong kind of attention. I attracted Frank Jones because I have such muscular legs. I asked him once why he married me. He said "Because you have such muscular legs. I thought you'd be good to have sons."

What was your favorite subject in high school and why?

Music... because I felt it. I felt music. I had to do the mental work with music because it came quite naturally with me whereas the subjects I had to work at. Although it was funny I had to work at algebra, but when we got to geometry I got all A's. It should be the other way around logically, but it wasn't with me. I did take typing and I made all three of my sons take typing in high school. The reason I told them was that typing would be of great value when they got out of high school and into college when you have so many papers to write. As soon as they took typing and passed the course I bought them a typewriter. They all had their own typewriter and they could all pick out the type they wanted as far as the print was concerned, the font. That's all I can think of really. My high school was rather boring.

Did you have a favorite teacher in high school?

I used to like Hargraves until that incident. Mrs. Robinson. In fact she was head of the music department, Mrs. Robinson and she was tough. But she was good. She demanded perfection from people and she got it. She didn't mind kicking you out if you didn't do the right thing. So as a result we had to do the right thing. We did the right thing. We had the right tones, right projections of voice and all sorts of things.

How did she influence you?

By demanding perfection within the vocal department. We had to have perfect pitch all the time and you had to do exactly what she told you or out you went. She used to sit beside me when we were watching. I used to have a little mole on the back of my neck. I haven't felt it for years. I haven't looked, maybe that's why. She used to sit there and put her arm around me and listen to what was going on. She wasn't paying attention to me really, but then she would be rubbing the mole with her finger at the same time [laughing].

I sang once in Lakme, the Bell Song from Lakme. Oh, it's a beauty, but it demands a high C. I used to be able to throw it out with no problem when I was young. I was doing it on the stage before the concert and so did Gertrude Babbitt. Well, Gertrude Babbitt was...we took voice from the same teacher and the teacher told me "Gertrude has a good voice, a very good voice, but the best she will ever do in life is direct the church choir." And that's exactly what she did. At the same time that he told me that about her, he said you have got the voice to go on and eventually be with the Metropolitan because I did have a good voice at one time, a very good and mature voice. But that's long gone and that's for several reasons. You have to use things and practice it and work at it and so on and so forth, learn languages. Anyway, he continued by saying "But I don't think you've got the drive to do what you have to do" [laughing]. And he was right. He was right on all parts.

Was religion an important part of your life during your teen years?

Not as much as it should be. But I did go to church now and then, but not every Sunday. I used to take the boys to church, Howard and Brian. Howard went more than anybody else. That's funny [laughs]. You see how much good it did. Of course, they didn't go to church. They went to the kindergarten within the church and that depends on the teacher. Actually, what they did is play games. They really don't study the bible or anything like that, very little.

Do you think Howard would have been different if he had studied the bible when he was little?

I think he would have had a better knowledge of what was what, but not necessarily any better. Howard has a mind of his own.

That's an understatement.

I know [both laugh].

Describe any part-time jobs you had in your teen years.

My first part-time job was at a five and ten cent store. When I was working there I had a crush on the floor walker. He was a young Chinese man that was partially crippled and I felt sorry for him. Of course that was just superficial and didn't last very long at all so he never knew anything about it. After that I started going with Frank.

I graduated and then I worked at Federal Department Store. That's where they did something that I later found out was illegal. Money was hard to get back then. That was in the early forty's before the war. This man, we used to have to take...he wanted to buy a shirt so he picked out the shirt and I said "We have to walk over to pay at the counter." So we walked over there and put the shirt down and I said "That will cost so much." He said "I gave you a twenty dollar bill." He didn't give me anything, but that was his way of getting a little extra money. He argued that he had given me a twenty dollar bill and the floor man naturally went along with him for reasons...he didn't even say "Well, the register should be twenty dollars short then" and check it out through that way. Instead they started taking it out of my pittance of a pay of three dollars a week so I got about two dollars a week. I decided it wasn't worth working there after about five weeks or something like that where they were automatically taking this money out of my pay and I quit. That's when I got a job at the telephone company. I was still in my teens, my late teens.

I was working at Federals, I told you, when Mr. and Mrs. Jones came in. Frank was in the army and she gave me this diamond, a very small diamond, but a diamond. It was small, about a third of a karat

It was probably the size of one of those...I don't know. I had it later, after the divorce, I took it and had it made into a necklace. It was white gold because Lucy was...or Amy was allergic to gold gold and I gave it to her when she was married. So where it is now I have no idea. I'm sure she sold it. That's her business. I also heard she's coming back to the states for a short visit.

Wait...who did you give it to, Lucy or Amy?

Her mother. It was Lucy.

So you gave your wedding ring to Lucy?

Uh huh. My engagement ring not the wedding ring. I think I just...I don't know what I did with that. It didn't have anything on it. It was chips. But then I told Amy that she should question her mother if she still has it just for the heck of it because that's where the diamond went. Amy didn't know anything about it naturally. I'm sure Lucy sold it, but that's for her find out if she's curious. If she isn't, so what? I thought maybe she might be lucky and inherit it. Not likely.

What were your favorite leisure activities?

Seizure?

Leisure.

Swimming. I still have the scar on my leg about that long. It's shrunken. That's why I won't dive into water anymore that I can't see. I haven't for years and years because I dove into the lake at Green Lake and somebody had broken a bottle and thrown it in on the bottom and when I curled to come up it just sliced me good. So I will not. I did not for years dive into water I could not see what was in it after that. During the teenage years, I assume?

Yes.

Sewing, of course. The woman here *[a resident at Desert Flower]* that used to make wedding gowns did it all by hand. You should see the suits she wears. It's amazing and she made them all. She used to work in a wedding shop. I decided that I couldn't sew next to her.

Describe your best friend during your teen years?

Jackie...what was her last name? I can't think of her last name. Her first name was Jackie.

Is that the one...was her name Newell?

No, huh uh, another one and I liked her very much and we were real close for ages, for a couple years and all of a sudden bingo. She wouldn't even speak to me. But she would never tell me why and to this I day I wondered why because it certainly wasn't anything I did. So the way I figured it somebody must have made up a story and told her out of jealousy or something. You know how kids are. But anyway, so she was my best friend for at least a couple of years. I gave you her name...no, it wasn't Jackie. It was Gertrude...Gertrude Babbitt.

And then what? We haven't gotten very far in that book.

I've been skipping back and forth and no, we haven't because there's a lot in it.

You're not kidding.

Are you getting tired of this?

No, it's just that I'm wondering...have I lived that much?

Of course you have. We'll skip the military section.

All right.

Where did you and your friends spend time and what did you do there when you were teenagers?

Everything we did we did together. Gertrude's father had died and her mother worked. He was alive when we first started our friendship, but then he had a heart attack and died. Her mother had to go to work so she was always alone after school. We would play games and we would chat about kids and people and so forth and so on. We would sing together. We would go to shows together. Do things like that together.

Was Gertrude at your fiftieth reunion?

No. She lived in California, but she's dead now. She died about eight, ten years ago.

How about your first date and your first kiss?

My first date, well I was thirteen years old [laughing]. I didn't get a kiss. In fact I walked home and left him there. He was the grandson of JC Penney and he thought he was King Tut. He took me to an ice cream social at the church, Episcopal Church and he just thought the girls should fall all over him. So that was my first date.

Later on I have to say my first date with Frank, we went to a show. He had to borrow his dad's car for Frank's friend to drive because Frank didn't have a driver's license yet at that point.

Another time I remember going to the great big theater. I don't remember what we saw, but it was that time of the month that very night. The first few days I always flowed extremely heavy, always and it lasted a week with me. At the show I wasn't about to cancel it, the date.

You were with Frank?

Yes, and there was another one. We took the bus to the theater and we had to take the bus home again. In the meantime, I overflowed, shall we say. And I had to take off my stockings because it ruined my stockings. I was so afraid that he would notice that I didn't have stockings on on the way home and I had them on when I went. If he did, he never said anything. I cleaned myself up and left my silk stockings, or rayon or whatever they were.

I remember another time Bill...I can't remember his last name. He asked me to go to the Detroit Symphony concert Sunday evening, free concert. So I went. I was sick, but I wasn't going to cancel out because I really liked him. He had a car and he drove and I swear I must have had pneumonia because I pooped. Oh, did I poop. During the show I'd cover my face, not the show, but the performance. I'd cover my face because I thought hopefully to muffle the pooping. But there's a big difference between coughing and pooping and I'm sure he wasn't very happy with it with his date either. He never asked me again. So anyway that was that time.

December 1, 2010

Tell me about your first steady boyfriend and how long you went together?

I didn't date a lot.

Where does the Plotz' person fit in all of this?

He was in the band, the orchestra and I went to a picnic with him. Every year the orchestra and the band had a big picnic at Rouge Park and Marion introduced me to Al. I really liked him, but he liked Marion. Everybody liked Marion and everybody liked Virginia, but I think Virginia was putting it out, but she would never admit it. Marion would say the same thing [Liz is giggling]. Anyway...what are you writing down?

I'm writing the date because when I put the tape back in here I want to have the right date on the label.

What were the most mischievous pranks you pulled?

I didn't.

Oh, come on! You didn't?

I'm serious. You know, I was an outcast in my family. Virginia and Marion were very close and Priscilla was much younger...about six years younger. I was just in the middle. Period. And I wasn't included in things. If they had fun or double dating or other things you know I just wasn't included [sounds sad]. I didn't date a lot. I think Mother thought that I was going to be with her for life [both laughing].

But then after Frank came in the picture he'd come over and we'd sit in the living room. Mother would sit in the kitchen or else upstairs in the bedroom. And while we were talking she was alright. But if we weren't talking she was afraid we were doing something we shouldn't do. So she'd say "Frank and Elizabeth, why don't you go downstairs to the recreation room. You could play the piano and so forth down there." We had an old player piano, pump piano with all the different rolls. So we went downstairs and about thirty minutes later she'd say "Elizabeth, why don't you and Frank come up here for a while. You must be getting tired down there." She had us running up and down the stairs. She wanted to keep me out of trouble [laughing]. Like there was going to be anything.

Well that kind of leads to the next question. What were the attitudes among teenagers about sex, smoking, drugs and alcohol?

Drugs weren't in the picture at that point. Alcohol I think was starting in the picture pretty good, but I don't know because I was never out with anybody that did those things. Smoking, drinking or what have you. Ralph...

What about the sex part?

What's that [teasing tone]? No, nothing.

Nobody talked about it?

Huh uh.

Except Virginia?

No, she wouldn't talk about it, but Marion knew something. Marion and Virginia were like two peas in a pod for years and then after she got I'm not sure which one, Virginia...they went on a double date. Marion and Virginia had a big row because Marion just could not agree with such things. She thinks Virginia...she's hinted strongly that Virginia put out with more than one, Paul Shuster, Tommy Moe and of course Harry. And to this day Virginia will tell you that...she won't tell you, but if you ask her she'll say well she didn't know what he was doing to her. He had pushed her up against a tree and did it to her there, just that one time. She got pregnant from just that one time and we're supposed to believe it. She didn't know what he was doing to her. Huh! She got that thing worn out from what I understand.

What kinds of things did you and your friends do on dates?

Held hands, he'd put his arm around the back of me, across my shoulders.

When you were at movies?

Typically, He usually held my hand at the movie. Frank...I don't think he had any girlfriends before me either. If he did it was only one or something. But he'd never admit to that. But I think when he got in the army he did some experimentation to see what life was all about. Huh! So what [laughs]?

Did you attend your school dances or proms and with who?

We didn't have any because the war was on.

What were some of the fads when you were a teenager?

Bell bottom pants. Everything makes a circle eventually.

Did you have them?

No, girls didn't wear pants back then.

So what were any girl fads?

Well, there were short dresses, but that was just above the knee. It wasn't up to just the girl's behiney.

Someone must have made a big complaint to the newscaster on Channel 10 the other night, the other day because the one day she had on a short skirt and she crossed her legs and she wiggled around and I mean she showed just about everything. I could tell you what color under panties she had on. For a newscaster, you know. But then the next day she had on a pants suit [giggles]. So she got repercussions somewhere along the line. She should have known better.

Describe the hair and clothing styles that were popular when you were a teenager.

Pageboy...I wore my hair in a pageboy at one time. I used to...my hair was real thick and I would have it trimmed to shoulder length almost...you know, shoulder length and then I would put a roller in periodically at night so that it would turn under. Then I would sleep in such a way that the roller didn't affect me. I always prided myself on the fact that I had a perfect roll all the way around.

Elizabeth's high school hair style

What did you like best and least about your appearance as a teenager?

Well, I compared myself with Marion and Marion was...she was very pretty. I think that's why Virginia did some of the things she did to be so popular because you know, Virginia...I never found her to be a pretty girl, ever. Whereas she wasn't bad looking or anything like that, but she was not pretty, but she was…compared to Marion she was not pretty at all. I compared myself with Marion too. Marion was tiny. She was petite and Marion loved to ride horses. She had a riding habit and boy she looked like a queen, a princess.

You didn't tell me what you liked best about you.

I said my hair. I had good legs and a small waist. I had a sixteen inch waist for a while, for I guess about a year. That's a pretty small waist.

Yes, it is.

In fact, between you and me when I retired or I was getting ready to retire from Consumers I had a proposal of marriage by a man that was ten years younger than I.

Why didn't you take him up on it?

No thank you. Two husbands is enough. Of course, I was…yes, I was married at that time.

To John?

Uh huh, when I retired. I was married in seventy five, retired in seventy nine.

This guy proposed to you and he knew you were married?

I said before I was married.

Oh, I thought you said . . .

Before I retired I meant to say. I meant to say before I was married, before I quit. Yes, Bob Breckenridge, but he knew I would not accept anyway because of the ten year difference.

Lucky you!

[Elizabeth laughs] I still had a decent figure back then. Sure went to pot after that.

What slang expressions were popular during your teen years?

I don't remember any. I'm not saying there weren't any. I'm just saying I don't remember any. I don't know.

What kind of music was popular and what was your favorite song?

Very often it was military or anything connected with the military because of the war being on… When Johnny Comes Marching Home, You've Gotta Get Up, Gotta Get up in the Morning, all of them. There were a couple of like… When I'm Calling You, Indian Love Call… a few of those… anything Nelson Eddy sang, Jeanette McDonald.

So what was your favorite or did you have a favorite song?

I don't know. I think it was Indian Love Call. That also, believe it or not, was Frank's… listen to me… John's Father's favorite song and he requested that be played at his funeral. So that we did.

Who was your favorite musical performer or band when you were a teenager?

Oh, Fred Astaire, Benny Goodman, all of those.

What kinds of dances were popular during your teen years?

[laughing as she answers] Let me see, of course I didn't go to dances. But let me see, we were still doing the waltz and the foxtrot and that stuff way back then too. That's when the...I can't think of the name of it...the ragtime type of thing. You stopped holding each other and you twirled around and got back together.

The jitterbug?

Yeah.

What was your favorite motion picture and why?

Oh, Nelson Eddy and Jeanette McDonald because he was always a gallant.

What movie was he in?

May Time, Rose Marie. I've got some of those on tape.

Describe your relationship with your parents. Were you able to communicate freely with them?

No.

Not when you were a teenager?

No, it was the generation thing. They were brought up where you didn't do those things and it just fell through, followed through I should say. The way they were, well then they treated their family that way. Daddy was more open than Mother was. But Mother's the one that went to different things with us. She took us to the art museum. She took us to Belle Isle. She did all of those things. Every year we would go to different things, different places in the Detroit area once she got a car.

How did you typically get in trouble with your parents and how were you punished?

I didn't typically do anything bad. It's like a parent's version of a child or a child's version of a parent version. They're always very, very different, you know.

So you didn't think you got into trouble?

It was always over Priscilla and the fact that she wore my clothes. My mother always took Priscilla's side.

Did she punish you or just make sure you let Priscilla wear the clothes?

I had to understand Priscilla. She looked out for Priscilla's feelings. But it was my clothes and my work that took care of them. I went to work and she stayed home.

Did you ever get in trouble in school?

Only if I didn't have as good a marks as my sisters had. And then dear Mrs. Jones, named apropos.

[After a very long pause] Always took Priscilla's side. I can't remember what side that was really. In Mother's eyes we had to understand her and I didn't understand her sleeping in her clothes at night and using mine in the morning.

Did you ever skip school?

Never.

Never?

Never.

Were you compatible with your siblings? Did you ever play tricks on them?

I was when we were younger. I would be the one that they would call upon if there was fresh snow on the roof and we would make ice cream out of it. But we had to wait until we had fresh snow and it was me that would go out and gather up the snow. I went out on the roof to gather the snow. They would tell me where it was…"over there, over yonder" so to speak. So they gave me the instructions and I wandered over the roof to gather the snow.

Oh, my! You actually really did get it off the roof?

Oh, yeah. I used to…my father used to say that he had the neighbors call them when they saw me out on the roof in the summer time even. I would go out there and walk around and jump off the roof. I remember it vaguely that he had them calling him to let him know I had done it or I was doing it. Virginia had me do a lot of dumb things. I was dumb enough to follow her desires.

Like what?

Like going out on the roof in the summer time and jumping off. That was her desire to see me do it and I guess I had too much fun doing it so I just did it on my own. So that's basically the snow story and the summer time story too. I forget that I'm talking into a machine.

When did you get your first car?

When I bought it… when I was… after Brian was born. I saved up…I think it was fifty-five dollars, either fifty or fifty-five dollars that I saved and I bought it from the neighbor that was selling it.

What was it?

It was a Dodge four-door. That's the one that Brian fell out of.

You got that for fifty-five dollars?

It was several years old when I got it. It was...it really did, it ran beautifully.

What color was it?

Blue. I had no proof of it misbehaving in any way when I took it out to the store or wherever.

What did you do in summers when there was no school or school was out?

I worked. I worked at Federals Department Store and that's where the man got a little extra money or to get some money period. He claimed he gave me twenty dollars when he didn't to get a shirt and I had to pay it back to Federals in three dollar amounts. They took it out of my weekly pay which left me about three dollars.

How old were you when you went to work at Federals?

How old was I? Wait a minute, the first job I had was at Federals Department Store...not Federals, it was a dime store, but I've forgotten the name of that and the second one was Federals. It was the first one at the dime store that I had a crush on the Chinaman. I felt sorry for him. He had one arm that was shorter than the other and I felt sorry for him basically. I had compassion for him.

Then I went to Federals Department Store and after that I got a job at the AT&T working nights. I worked nights because I made more money that way. I liked working nights because I was the only person working on the ninth floor in solitary and I had to lock the door after me at night. Supposedly it was information that could be dangerous because it was a lot of chit chat from one soldier to another soldier during the war.

I took a street car and I feel asleep all the time on that street car and it woke me up at Wonder Bread Baking Company. The odor of the bread being baked had a tendency to wake me up. Then I would stay awake until I got to my stop. I walked three long blocks to get home and I got off at five o'clock in the morning. I started at eleven.

You had a six hour shift?

But I made more money for working at night.

Did you accomplish something in your teens of which you are very proud?

I won the Michigan Division prize for being the best female twirler in Michigan.

What was your greatest fear when you were a teenager?

It wasn't a fear it was...actually well, maybe it was, of not being liked. I wanted to be liked to make up for my lack of ability to live up to my sisters...their record of ability. When I got into high school it developed more.

To whom did you turn for advice?

I didn't have anyone [sounds sad]. I really didn't have anyone that I turned to for advice.

Is that why you're so strong now, because you had to depend on yourself?

It's possible. It's very possible.

Whom did you admire the most as a teenager?

Gertrude Babbitt.

Why?

Because she had such a good voice and she's the one I told you about that we took from the same teacher.

Who influenced you most during your teen years?

Dear old Mr. Hargraves. He was head of the band and the orchestra and of course, he was also the one that took advantage of me.

But he influenced you as well?

Before...you know I had four years of high school so that I had four years of being influenced.

Tell the story about something funny or embarrassing that happened to you as a teenager?

Well, when I played with the Detroit Symphony Orchestra I was eighteen or nineteen, one or the other...eighteen, I think. I had an audition that I passed to be selected in the A orchestra. They had an A and a B orchestra, the City did and I was in the A orchestra, of course. So that first day I auditioned and I went to rehearsal and then before the concert we had a rehearsal before the audition. We had a rehearsal before the concert is the way I should put it. So I had on my black and white evening dress that Virginia had passed down to me. I loved that evening dress. That was another one that somebody has of me that Virginia passed down to me. Somebody has that.

They have the dress itself or a picture of you in it?

A picture of me in it. I was at the rehearsal chewing gum and Mr. Kolar who was the director of the symphony at that time stopped the rehearsal and said "Would the girl back there in the checkered white dress and chewing gum please spit the gum out and dispose of the gum?" I don't remember how he worded it. It made me feel very, very small, very tiny, very inadequate to be there.

Oh, dear.

There's a picture of me in the orchestra and it shows me with that dress on. I was way back in the back, not one of the prominent ones. I had my purse with me and I had to get a Kleenex to spit the gum out in. It was embarrassing. Everyone turned around to look to see who the girl was in the orchestra.

Elizabeth playing in the Detroit Symphony Orchestra in 1940 (visible in the last seated row left side of group)

That would be memorable.

Yes.

Did you have a nickname?

Beth. I had the nickname of Beth. Al Plotz to the day he died called me Beth because in high school he always called me Beth. You could tell if people went to high school with me by what they called me.

How did you become such good friends with Al Plotz's mother?

I had looked him up and he had an apartment up over there in their house on the second floor. They made it into an apartment for him and then all he had to do was go in the garage and go down Michigan Avenue to the library where he worked. He was in charge of all of that, all of the work for the library. He was the number one man. Of course I was over there and I met him through high school and I met her through him living with his parents. Not with them, but in the apartment over them.

When he died I was the first person to know about it. I went over there and was greeted at the door with "Didn't you know that Al had been murdered?" And she proceeded to tell me. And I didn't know, of course because it happened the night before and I hadn't read a paper. I had to find out by just going over there and being greeted at the door and her telling me about it. Instead of me consoling her she consoled me. He was lying in what had been the dining room in a hospital bed because he had osteosarcoma which killed him, cancer of the bone.

This was Al's father?

Yeah. He made the statement that if he had been a young man I wa the type of girl that he would have liked to have married and I thought he shouldn't have said that in front of her.

I turned that off for a minute so I can hear you better. I can hardly hear you. Who was the president of the United States when you were in high school and what do you remember about him?

Did you want me to turn off the heat because the cooler, the air conditioner went off and we should open the window?

So is it too hot?

Yeah.

Okay, I'll turn it back on, but you have to talk louder.

Who was the president? Was it Truman?

I don't know. When you were in high school...what year?

Oh, in high school?

Yes.

Well gee, I don't know for sure, but it seems to me it was Truman, it seems to me.

No, I don't think so because...wasn't Truman...well, I guess he could have been.

I don't know.

[Franklin Roosevelt was president when she was in high school].

December 8, 2010

It's still warm in here, isn't it?

It's okay.

I can turn that down.

No, it's okay because it makes lots of noise and plus it's plenty warm in here. I just turned off the fan and we're okay.

Oh, you put that there.

I did, but you can sit back for a minute.

I thought that was something else.

Nope. Do you want me to help you?

No. The P.T. (physical therapy) man had me walk the whole perimeter up here and go downstairs, go downstairs and then go outside and walk the perimeter of the... of the...

The building?

The garden. It's decorated and so that it was... I came back up, walked back up to see my endurance.

Was this with or without your walker?

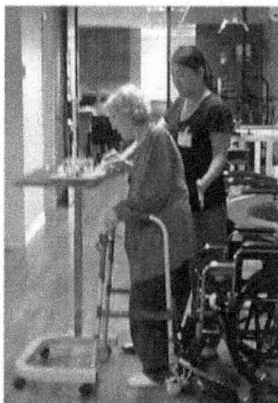

No quit in her - rehab after the 1st hip break

Without...or with, I'm sorry. Yes and he said I did very well. He was testing my endurance. So that anyway, shall we go?

Sure. I'll sit it right there.

What were the most important things you had learned about life by the time you reached middle age?

And what is middle age?

Forty to sixty-five.

That I should have divorced Frank many years before. Like my boys said and Brian said that if I had divorced dad a lot earlier then I would have somebody that was a father more than Frank was. So that that was the most, strongest thing that he said, the boys said. Howard didn't say that, but Brian did. Brian was quite verbal about that. In fact, when he heard that we were getting a divorce he cried and so that at any rate, that's basically what I learned...that I should have done it sooner, much sooner.

Between the ages of forty and sixty-five what was the best year for you and why?

Well, they were all good years because John was a special person and I had to be careful because if I said I saw something in the stores that I liked I'd have to be careful because I would find it in the house the next day or two.

How old were you when you married John?

Fifty-five.

What was the worst year and why...between ages of forty and sixty-five?

The best year, I should add to that. The best year was the year I got the divorce. When I walked out of the divorce court I felt like I just had a fresh shower and all the world was nice and shiny and bright and clean,

As far as the worst year is concerned, the worst year, the worst year was when...I just have to say the worst year was when...it's hard to say. I really didn't have any worst years after that. Except that when they said that, they said that Howard had...John had about seven weeks to live. Of course, if he had radiation he could live longer, but really that's about it.

When did you discover that you were middle-aged [laughing because of the look on her face]?

When did I discover I was middle-aged?

Yep.

I have to say when I lost John and I was alone after that.

How old were you when John died?

Let's see. We were married twenty-three years. When John died, oh my, that would have been...twenty-three. Huh. Fifty-three, sixty-three, seventy-three...I would have been seventy-seven when I discovered that John was dying.

Seventy-seven or sixty-seven?

Seventy-seven.

You were seventy-seven?

Well, it...

Didn't John die in ninety-seven?

Yeah. He was seventy-six when he died and so that I was four years younger.

So you were seventy-two?

I would have been in my seventies, you see.

In your middle years how did you prefer to spend your leisure time?

We liked to fly, we liked to sail. We liked to just do things together.

Did you also spend a lot of time playing your cello?

Yes.

How old were you when you first started going to Pingree?

The first year I went was it was...ninety-three? No, that's not right. I have to get a calculator.

Although she flew a number of planes, her favorite was always their classic J-3 Cub

That's all right. What are you calculating?

The fact that he was seventy-six, I was seventy-four and that's when I stopped going to Pingree.

When? When he was sick you stopped going?

No, I still went when he was sick.

Well, you even went after he died though because you went when you lived in Show Low for a few years. You moved to Show Low when you were seventy-three.

That would be about it.

How was your relationship with your children during your middle years?

It was...

[Laughing] You make such funny faces. You're cute.

When they were, we weren't close because Howard...everybody lived away. Brian lived fairly close. The first year after John died I went over and spent Christmas time after... Brian... Christmas. I was never close with Jeff. I was never as close with Jeff as I was the other boys.

Why do you think that is?

Well, he had his boyfriends and girlfriends.

I thought the first year after John died you drove to Arizona and you spent Christmas with us.

I stopped going to Arizona in ninety-three.

You stopped going to Arizona in ninety-three?

I mean to Pingree.

In ninety-three?

Uh-huh.

You stopped or you started going?

Boy, my brain...

Two-thousand six was the last year you went to Pingree because that was the year you got the shingles and so you never went to Pingree again after that.

You're right.

John died in nineteen-ninety seven, he died in August and you came to our house for Thanksgiving that year and you stayed there until the end of January of ninety-eight.

You're right.

Then you came back to Charlevoix and sold your house and packed up all your stuff and shipped it to Arizona.

That's true. Very true.

The year you turned seventy-four you were living in Arizona and you drove to Pingree. The year you turned seventy-four you were still going to Pingree and that was ninety-eight. So you went for a long time. You went for thirteen years to Pingree.

He told me to keep going as long as I could go and so I did.

Well, it was probably a welcome vacation for you.

Yes, it was. It seems hot in here.

Do you want me to turn the air conditioning on?

It's pretty well on.

What was your relationship with your parents during your middle years?

Like when Howard was young he got the measles or mumps and Mother came over with groceries.

But that's not your middle years. When you were forty to sixty-five what was your relationship like with your parents? How old were you when your mother passed away?

I would have been, let's see.

Do you remember what year she died?

She was eighty-six when she died and she was born in ninety-eight. I mean in ninety-nine...eighteen ninety-nine.

So she died in nineteen eighty-five. So you would have been sixty-one. So in those years when you were forty to sixty-one years old what was your relationship like with your mom?

Well, I didn't let Mother know that I had a problem in my marriage because Marion and Virginia both were getting divorced.

Marion?

I mean Priscilla and Virginia both were getting a divorce and they were very verbal about it. So that I felt that Mother and Daddy had enough problems without me chiming in with mine. So that I never let them know it until after I was divorced. I was divorced when I was fifty-five.

You got along with your parents or you didn't?

Yes, very much. Daddy came to me when Mother accused him of having an affair which he didn't. He would come over and verbally cry to me about Mother and her accusations and that was after Marion died of course. I mean that was after Priscilla took off. I gave her my share of the car and she didn't have a car or anything. She went through the money that Marion and I gave her like water after Mother died. I can't remember what year. Virginia would know.

Are you glad or sad that you gave her your share of the money?

Oh, I was pleased.

But in hindsight after she went through it were you still pleased?

Yes, I was disappointed that she didn't use it properly. But she never used money properly. Priscilla was one that was always you know, money went through her fingers like water, always.

What were your strengths and weaknesses during your middle years?

My strengths and weaknesses were the fact that I kept my business, my personal business to myself.

That was your strength?

Uh-huh. And my weakness was that I wasn't more like Katie.

In what way?

Well, she bossed him. She put him in situations where he couldn't get out of.

And what do you think would have happened if you had been more like Katie?

I probably would have stayed married, but it would have continued an unhappy marriage so it wasn't a good thing. My weakness was the fact that I let Frank control me.

How was your relationship with John? How was that different because of your relationship with Frank? Did you treat John differently that you treated Frank?

No, John was different. When the checks came in he handed them to me. So at first I felt kind of strange taking them. But he wanted me to handle the money so I did.

Well, don't you think that you didn't need to be different either, that you just maybe got married to the wrong man and there wasn't a thing wrong with you at all?

That's very true.

You didn't need to change to fit him. That would have been a bad thing for you to do, I think.

That's very true. I married too young to know what I needed for a lifetime partner.

Oh, we've all made that mistake [laughing].

Oh, well. We learned from it.

John wouldn't have been available for you because he was married to someone else at first too.

Yes, uh-huh. His wife died. That's why he became available.

Did you suffer any financial or emotional losses during your middle years?

No. I didn't have the money to do it with.

So that was financial, but didn't you suffer emotional loss through your marriage to Frank or you didn't?

No.

You didn't feel like that was an emotional loss?

No.

What did you fear the most during the middle years?

Frank because he was so…he controlled me by emotionally controlling me that way. He didn't give me anything to handle and he was very verbal against anything I did. Anything I did was never good enough so that…this chair is hot. Wow.

Do you want to sit on the couch? I'll scoot over and you can come and sit over here.

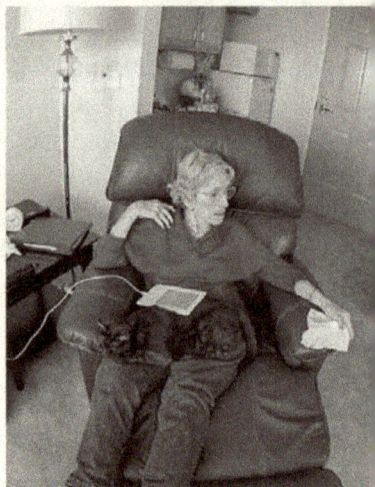

When Howard and I brought Elizabeth to Scottsdale from San Diego to reside in an assisted living facility, we rented a van so we could bring some of her favorite things. One of those was a big brown leather recliner. She loved to sit in that chair and watch television. In Scottsdale she would sit in it with her cat on her lap while I interviewed her.

Ready for the interview - sitting in her favorite chair with her best friend on her lap. This photo was taken in her new "apartment" in Scottsdale a few weeks before she died.

Did you experience changes in your physical well-being in your middle years?

My physical well-being?

Did you have any surgeries?

Yes, I had breast surgery and I remember when I found it, it wasn't cancer it was tumors, fibroid tumors. Well then I was ready to come home and I called Frank and asked him to come and take me home and he said "I'm too busy. Get Priscilla to come and get you". It was that type of thing, the physical thing.

What about your knee?

That was after I was married with John.

Yes, but you weren't sixty-five were you when you fell and broke your knee. How old were you?

Yes, because we had the place out overlooking Lake Michigan. So I definitely was married to John when I did that to myself.

Yes, but your middle years overlap Frank and John. Do you remember how old you were when you did that to yourself?

Probably about fifty-eight, about that age.

That was a nasty thing, wasn't it?

Yes, it was. He wheeled me around in a wheel chair and he would tell people "I told her not to bungee jump", things like that. He always made a joke out of things.

Did you have a mid-life crisis?

No, I can't say I did.

How did your values, goals and priorities change?

They did after the divorce.

What were your values after the divorce?

He didn't want me to go to work. He was afraid that I would have money and he wouldn't be able to control me as often and as much. Basically that was it. I went ahead and put my application in regardless and when they called me well I danced around the kitchen and it was one of the happier days of my existence. I felt that I was worthwhile again.

How old were you when you got that job?

I had to have been about fifty-two, fifty-three, in that area.

What became more important to you after that?

The feeling of independence and boy I enjoyed that work.

What was the most significant realization you came to during your middle years?

After I went to work I found that they would pay for my education as long as I was there in the business area. I continued to go to college and had good marks and it made me feel that I was worthy of something.

And you hadn't felt like that for a long time?

No, huh uh.

What classes were you taking?

I took everything from English to psychology, what you'd take the first couple of years.

Did you get a degree?

I got an Associate Degree.

Good for you.

I got almost all A's. I got one B plus.

That's cool.

Yes, it made me feel worthy.

All that time they were telling you that you couldn't compete with Virginia and Marion and it was only because you weren't trying.

That's right. I know when Frank and I were getting a divorce and I told him what I would do to settle the divorce he said "Who told you that? You're too stupid to do it yourself." He was still trying to slap me down.

What do you believe to be your most important accomplishments in mid-life?

Being good enough to play in the symphonies that I played with.

What was the best part of being middle-aged?

In her later years, she not only played in the Silver Creek Symphony, she played at various charity events

Being married to John [laughing].

Is there anything else you'd like to share about your middle years?

Of course flying was quite an accomplishment.

Well, yes that was. The best part of being middle-aged wasn't being able to do as you damn well pleased and not having to answer to anybody and not have kids in the way? That's what I think now that I'm middle-aged [laughing]. It's kind of nice not having to be responsible for anybody.

Well, yes, that's true.

Is there anything else you want to share about your middle years?

I guess not.

How did you feel upon becoming a senior citizen?

It didn't bother me except when I got into my eighties. I really didn't feel old until I got in my eighties.

Why does that make you feel old?

Just walk around down stairs and you'll know what I mean. [By "down stairs" she means the facility she was living in at the time. There were many people who were lots older than her and in need of lots of help].

Yes, but you weren't feeling good? Is that it?

No, although that's part of it. It's the realization that you don't have many years left.

Have your senior years been like you always thought they would be?

Except for the last two or three years.

Well, you've been on a tough ride. You have.

Yep.

The shingles were a life-changing event for you.

Yep.

That was a tough, tough deal.

You're right.

I think you're still paying for those shingles.

I know I am [laughing].

It changed a whole lot for you to have those. You ended up in all that pain.

I still have it.

I know it and that's a long time to feel that way.

December 15, 2010

Tell about how and when you decided to retire.

When I was first able to do so.

How old were you?

Fifty-five...But I didn't retire though until I was fifty-nine because I couldn't retire before then or else I wouldn't have gotten any pension at all.

That pension's been nice, don't you think?

It's been mine.

I said it was nice.

Yes, but it's small.

Well it may have been small, but it was something for all your work you did.

Yes, it is true.

What hobbies did you take up after retiring?

Sewing. I bought a new machine which I had wanted for some time.

Anything else? Is that when you took up the flying too or did you do that before you retired?

On the other question, when I was young, but I took it up when I was with children and not having a cello and everything. Frank would never buy me one. So I felt that I lost a lot of years and I did.

Well, you don't play like you lost a lot of years. You must have caught yourself right up because you play very nicely.

Thank you, but I didn't. I did much better in my younger years.

I'm sitting on something. Oh, it's your glasses case. Oh, my god, let's get rid of that cat fur.

What did I do with that?

What misconceptions do people have about being a senior citizen?

That you have enough to fill your time. They seem to think that you sit around and do nothing, that you don't have enough things to occupy your time.

You always had plenty. You did the sewing. You did sailing. You flew planes. You did your cello.

I did flying.

Yes, you did lots of things.

Uh-huh.

What is your favorite joke about the golden years?

Joke?

Yes.

Although she and John had a 40 foot motor-sailor, her favorite boat was always her Sunfish. She spent hours solo-sailing on Lake Michigan.

You just spoke of it…that you don't have enough to fill your time and that's a joke. People seem to think that you do nothing but sit around.

Do you feel you've attained a certain wisdom with age?

Oh, yes. Uh-huh…certain wisdom that I should have gotten divorced much sooner.

Well, at least you did it when you did it and you can't fix that now.

Yes, I know. I can't do that.

Have you become emotionally stronger with age?

Oh, yes.

Can you explain?

Emotionally stronger I am because I am. People don't pull the rug over my eyes the way they would have when I was younger. The way they did when I was younger.

Have you lost many loved ones?

Lost? To what reason?

I'm assuming death. It doesn't say, but that's my assumption of what they're asking.

Well, then I say it was just one and that was Al Plotz.

I think they're defining loved ones as anyone you may have loved like your parents or anybody that you might have lost, siblings.

All of my family members as there are only one left out of six. So you would have to say there is only one out of six left.

But you were referring to Al Plotz or Mrs. Plotz?

I said Al Plotz. I didn't add Mrs. Plotz, but I should have. There's only two on that side. I didn't count Mr. Plotz because I didn't know him long enough before he died. But Mrs. Plotz was a dear, dear lady and of course Al was very much like his mother.

And John? Would you put John in there?

No, I didn't count him as family yet I should have. I certainly should have.

How have their losses affected you?

Well, it makes you sorry that you didn't do some things and that you did other things. You'll always feel a great loss.

Have you remained healthy into your golden years?

Healthy? Until I was in my seventies...at least into my seventies because I didn't know that I had hepatitis C.

What is the best part about being a senior citizen?

Oh, you can say things and do things that you wouldn't dare say when you were younger.

It's cool that you can get away with that [laughing].

You can.

What is the worst part of being a senior citizen?

Well, if you end up with disease, that's not good. Or if you're dumb enough to grab a cat and jump out of bed and break a hip. You do have a tendency to think that nothing's going to bother you. You're just going to live forever so to speak.

That's a good attitude to have though.

And the trouble is you don't and you find the end.

don't know though. You've done pretty well even after you broke your hip. I'm sure it hasn't been a lot of fun, but for lots of people, that is the beginning of the end and you fought yourself right back.

A lot of people call it the beginning of the end.

They do because they can never, ever recover from it and you did. It probably hurt like hell and you didn't care sometimes.

have to admit that it did.

You are strong, I'm telling you. What changes should be made to benefit senior citizens?

By the public in general?

guess, or maybe government changes. I don't know.

Well, it would be nice to say that you didn't have to bother with paying insurance anymore, but that's kind of ridiculous. My mother believed that. When she turned eighty she quit paying and they never checked her out. But then when she died I realized that she didn't have enough to make it to the government's benefit to go after her because she didn't have that much in savings.

So they left you alone?

Yes.

Have you been discriminated against or treated unfairly because of your age?

I don't think so.

If you want to know the honest truth I think at your age you've gotten a lot of benefits because you know how to work it. You've gotten all these young men to help you at stores and all kinds of things. They're not discriminating. They're helping [laughs].

But it's insulting sometimes [both laughing].

Yes, but I've seen you ask for the help and not be insulted.

Yes, well that's the way it should be. You should be left alone unless you ask for help.

Does being a senior offer any special opportunities or privileges?

Yes. People have a tendency to let you get ahead in line when there is a line.

That's nice.

Sometimes it's the opposite. They look at you as a stumbling block. You're holding them up. But most of the time people are very nice.

Do you feel people today give seniors the respect they deserve?

And don't deserve sometimes. I know I've come across quite a few seniors that don't deserve the respect that they get because they are demanding and mean.

During your golden years have you played an important role in the lives of your grandchildren?

I don't know. I think I have as far as Brian's are concerned. I haven't been around Tempest enough to really say. Although I've been around her and I feel that I'm closer to Tempest by far than I am to Chelsea just because of her parents holding her back.

Well, I think you've played an important role in the lives of Brian's girls and in Tempest's.

I don't know how I did with Frank. I don't know how anybody can with Frank.

Are any of your looks, personality traits or talents evident in your grandchildren?

Well, Brian's children sometimes show the same type of care and love that Brian shows. So that I can't say that they got that from me. But they do show it.

Why can't you say they got it from you?

Because they got it from their dad, who in turn got it from me.

Okay, there you have it. Well, I think you have one granddaughter that is the spitting image of you when you were her age.

Is that Leslie?

Yes. Don't you think she favors you a lot?

Uh-huh.

I look at her and say "Whoa, she looks just like Elizabeth." That picture that Tella sent…that could have been Leslie sitting there.

There is quite a resemblance, that's true.

I think Brian looks more like you than Howard and Jeff do.

Yes, that's true.

Is there anything else you would like to say about your golden years?

Well, there are more positives than there are negatives.

Name some positives things from right now right at this point in your life.

I can speak out and express my feelings. I couldn't do that when I was young.

That is a positive to be able to express how you really feel.

Yes, it's definitely a positive.

What is your ethnic origin?

My mother's side is mostly German although there's quite a bit of English in there. My father's side is strictly English with one exception and he used to rub it into my mother just because he knew it irritated her [laughing].

What is that exception?

But she laughed at it. There's a black Irish in there. I don't mean black Irish. I meant black...I don't mean black color.

What does your ethnic and cultural background mean to you?

Well, it I had to define it I would say that it really doesn't mean a great deal, but it...I have pride in it, though like you feel toward your Irish relatives. I feel that way towards the English and the German.

Do you like German food and the English food?

I like the English food better than the German food. The English I think are more bland in their choice of food than the Germans are.

I think you're right. They're not very creative, are they?

No.

What are the most important holidays celebrated as part of your ethnic heritage?

Well, Christmas, of course. As to the ethnic heritage I can't say we celebrate anything really that is strictly part of our heritage.

We never... although I used to go with John to the German club. We had a lot of fun dancing and so forth. He was a lot of fun to go to a party with because there was no end to his energy when it came to dancing and when I got tired...of course it wasn't too long after I had the knee operation. I would ask to sit down and he'd say "Sure, but do you mind if I ask the ladies to dance that don't have a partner? I've noticed some that don't have a partner." And he did that. He picked on the older ladies.

Do you miss dancing?

No, not anymore. I was never a good dancer, but Marion was. I guess Virginia was too. But I was never...I didn't date as young as they did, either.

So you think that was why they were better dancers?

Well, it contributed, uh-huh.

How do you feel about maintaining a strong identity to your ethnic and cultural heritage?

Well, we've been…My mother's family was in this country for so many years back before the Revolutionary war so that really didn't stand out as something that we would celebrate every year.

Is a certain religious denomination associated with your ethnic group?

Well, it was Protestant. Protestant all the way back as far as I know and the only thing Daddy ever said was it would hurt him if one of his girls changed…how did he word it? He worded it in such a way that they had to stay within the church to make him…he thought that they should stay within the church because of his upbringing. He was a minister.

He didn't know about Marion, did he?

No, and Marion hid It well from Daddy. But he said that as long as they stayed within the Protestant church, it didn't matter which one, but it would hurt him if they married outside of the Protestant church. In other words, if maybe they married Jewish. But that's the only thing he ever said.

What famous members of your ethnic group do you admire the most?

Well, let's see. I used to know some names, but they've evaded me now.

Have you been to your ancestral land? Have you been to England or Germany?

Yes. I've been to both England and Germany.

And what did those trips mean to you?

Well, it was interesting to me. I didn't feel related to it. I didn't feel connected to it.

Did you think you might before you went?

No, I didn't. If I did at all it was England.

You felt more connected to England than Germany?

I think so.

When you were growing up what were the things your parents told you about people outside your ethnic group?

Well, I should be against the Gypsies. Of course when the Second World War came along…it was probably the same as the First World War, but you know I wasn't around to notice that she was definitely…she denied her German connection.

Your mother?

Uh-huh, but when you read that book Howard has you see a strong connection there. But they were adamant about marrying outside of the Christian family and that went with the…although they would have accepted it they would have been against it too if one of us had married Catholic.

How do you feel about marriage outside your ethnic group?

It didn't bother me, but it did my mother. It bothered my mother very much.

How would she have felt if you had married outside your ethnic group?

For many, many years she was definitely against it. And Cliff's daughter married black, you know.

Was your mother still alive when that happened?

Yes.

And how did that go over?

Not well at all. And Virginia was definitely against it. She said that he would not be allowed in her house.

What would you have done if one of your son's had married a black woman?

I would have been unhappy about it, but I would have welcomed them.

What if they had married an Italian?

Same thing.

Well, you had a son that married a Native American and a Mexican [laughing].

Yes, I know.

And how did you feel about it?

I participated in the wedding.

In both weddings?

In one.

When he married Roberta?

No, when he married the Indian girl.

Yes, that's Roberta.

Roberta, yes. It's kind of hard to remember all of them [both are laughing hard].

So you went to the reservation for the wedding?

Yes.

And how did you feel about that?

Well, I thought "If Howard's happy, I should be happy for him." That's the way I felt.

Did you spend very much time around Roberta?

Elizabeth participating in a traditional Navajo wedding ceremony in 1980.

Not a lot, just when I visited then I did. Right off the bat I picked up on the fact that the women run the household, the Navajo people. She found that he was running around. I shouldn't tell this now. Then she came to me and told me about it as if I was the controller. I was the older controller. Therefore I ruled the roost and I could tell him to stop and he should stop, you know. That's the way they run. The oldest woman is the ruler.

What did you say to her?

Well, I didn't realize it at the time that this was so strong in the Navajo people. It was after that that I learned very quickly that the women ruled the roost and that's the way it was. When you marry a

Navajo, that's part of the make-up that you have to adopt. You know how that would go with Howard [both laughing].

Tell me about the first time you became aware of ethnic prejudice.

It was through my mother. She was very strong in this area against the blacks. And yet also she was...when Virginia was in high school, Virginia was going with Tommy Nokes and she liked him very much and Mother was afraid she would run off and marry him. He was from England, but Mother didn't know where he was from. Had she known, she probably would have accepted him.

He was black?

No.

He wasn't black; he was just a foreigner?

Uh-huh. He was always meticulously dressed and everything. But Mother was just afraid of losing Virginia early.

How old was Virginia?

She was about sixteen, seventeen at the most.

Is there a particular incident of ethnic prejudice that stands out in your memory?

Well, that probably is it. It was Tommy Nokes. Mother was afraid Virginia would run off and marry him and beyond that point it was always a reference to the blacks and particularly when a black family moved in across the street. It showed a great deal. But you know, they had a teen aged boy and he was so nice and so nice to Mother that I swear he changed her mind. She became very much...she liked the blacks after that, it seemed.

How old were you when that happened?

I was married at that point. Priscilla, oh she was terrible, just terrible. I remember when Daddy had his first heart attack. He was in the Highland Park Hospital and we were over there. It was the night time and we were leaving to go home and there was a black fellow walking toward us on the same side of the street. And she said…I can still see her hands. She said "What are you doing? You should be on the other side of the street when we're walking here." And she went like that to him and she said "Get away. Go away." She hated the blacks because they were black. She would have a hard time today, I tell you.

You mean with the President?

Even before that because there are so many blacks in Detroit and all over. Here you see the black women working with their burkas. I think that's what they're called. [At Desert Flower where Elizabeth was staying there were several Muslim women who worked there]. She would have a hard time adjusting to it. In her mind she was far superior and they shouldn't even be on the same street with her.

And how did you feel about that?

I was embarrassed, very embarrassed. But nobody was going to change her, that's for sure.

Sadly, this was my last interview with Elizabeth. Howard and I had to return to San Diego on December 17, 2010. We arrived back in Scottsdale on January 26, 2011. On February 5, 2011 Elizabeth fell while undressing after having dinner with her son Jeff and his wife, Judy. She broke her other hip. A few days after surgery she suffered a stroke. Elizabeth died on Valentine's Day, February 14, 2011 under the care of Hospice of the Valley.

My first introduction to Elizabeth was by telephone in early 1984. Howard and I had been dating for about four months and he decided to call her so the two of us could talk. I will never forget the first thing she ever said to me. "Did Howard tell you that he is going to take care of me when I get old?" It was a little bit of a surprise question and I replied "No, he didn't, but what a nice thing for him to do." Elizabeth never forgot that Howard had made that promise to her. When she was unable to function without some help she moved in with us for about three months until we could locate a condo a few blocks from our house. This allowed her to keep her independence. Helping Elizabeth in her later years was an experience I will always treasure.

Appendix A

For a period of about 10 years, I wrote a newspaper column in Arizona (under a pen-name) that carried a touch of a political bent. It was controversial, but every now and again, a topic came to the fore that was different. My mother's near death experience in 2006 was one of those topics. What follows is the verbatim text of a column published in late 2006.

Don't get your hopes up. This has nothing to do with anything coming from the White House; some things are beyond miracle. But I'll confess *54 Candles* is almost always rooted in truth, but just for the sport of it all, there's usually a little color added if for no other reason than to annoy you. Call it literary license; that would be the most flattering term. However, this missive is unusual in that there is nothing but hard, absolute fact. Not only a first, but hopefully a last.

A drunken motorcyclist speeding along at 100 miles-per-hour struck the car my mother was driving. It was a head-on squarely between her headlights. The call came to me around midnight. I was told she was hospitalized and probably wouldn't survive the night. I rushed the seventy miles to the hospital. Somehow, through a combination of intestinal fortitude and stubbornness she survived the accident. What we didn't know at the time was the accident was to ultimately take her life. In one of her many transfusions lurked the deadly hepatitis virus. That was 1972.

Hepatitis ultimately attacks the liver and so it did my mother's a couple of weeks ago. Sheriff's officers found her dying and rushed her to the hospital. Her condition was beyond critical and she was flown to Mayo. I got the call, just like the one in 1972. "She might not make it." Again I rushed to the hospital as did my brother. My brother and I arrived at the airport, caught a cab and set out for the ICU. As we rounded the corner into the darkened hospital room, the scene was reminiscent of a 30's vintage Lon Cheney film. It was apparent we might be seeing our mother for the last time.

For more than a week, she laid in her bed, medically "unresponsive". Her life was slowly fading away with each pulse of the machine that pumped fluids into her body. With every passing day, hope spoke with a softer and more distant voice. Finally, my brother had to return to his home a couple thousand miles distant. He said his final tearful good-bye to his mother and I took him to the airport.

The following morning, I reflected on my mother's life. Her existence had always been centered on her music. She'd played cello for a symphony orchestra of great renown back east and continued to play her instrument into her 83rd year. Although I had no way of knowing if she could hear anything as she teetered on the brink of death, I somehow felt it appropriate to push the rules a bit. I "smuggled" a mandolin into the hospital. I sat in her room and quietly played many of the songs she'd loved for years. I paused and a nurse said, "Please don't stop. Didn't you see how her face relaxed as soon as you began playing?"

I'd been playing for more than an hour when a team of three doctors arrived and asked to meet with me. I was told hope was gone. According to my mother's living will, she was not to be kept alive artificially. If we were to remain true to her wishes, we had to face the reality that it was time to remove her from life-support systems and let nature take its course. Although I was the one with the legal authority and moral obligation to make that dreadful decision, I told the doctors I wanted to speak with my brother and my mother's sister before doing so. I left the hospital and sadly made the calls. We agreed that it was time to honor my mother's wishes and remove her from life support. No one wanted her to suffer unnecessarily and her dignity was not to be compromised.

I returned to the hospital. It was time to do what my brother had done before me and say my final good-bye to my mother. The sense of dread weighed a thousand pounds as I rounded the corner and entered her room. Can you imagine my shock when I looked and there she sat, upright, eyes wide open? "Well, Hello there" she said. "How are you?"

It was as if she'd been raised from the dead. She was quite alert. Her memory was fine. As you might expect, she was a bit tired physically, but after having been tied in a bed for eight-days, I would have expected nothing else. She wanted me to play more music. I continued to play for another three hours until my fingers blistered. She settled back down for a much needed nap.

As she dozed off, I could only wonder if I'd just witnessed the "rally before the end" or a genuine recovery. The following morning as I prepared to go to the hospital for the answer, the phone rang. My heart dropped when I found it was someone from the hospital. Much to my amazement, the voice said "We're discharging your mother today."

She's now in a rehabilitation center and doing very well. I've finally got a chance to get back home and tend to matters ignored for the past couple of weeks. As I depart, the mandolin remains with my mother. I bet she knows how to play it when I get back in a few days. You can believe what you want. It could have been nothing more than coincidence. Or it could have been an incredible demonstration of the power of music. Or something else. The medical team at Mayo believes it was the music. I can only say that whenever I feel afraid, I whistle a happy tune.

Appendix B

The following is the text of the obituary I was asked to write for a newspaper. It summarizes the life of a woman with true grit and that never stopped "growing up" until the day she died.

Goodbye to the Toughest Lady

Light snow was falling. Driving conditions were becoming dangerous more than 9,000 feet high in the Rockies. She'd been on the road for more than sixteen hours. Her lifelong friend sat quietly in the passenger seat as she drove from Show Low, Arizona to Bellvue, Colorado. Her cello would sing with its deep, dark, haunting voice soon enough when they finally arrived at the Pingree Park Campus of Colorado State University where they attended a weeklong music camp every year. What seventy-five year old woman would drive nearly 1,700 miles round trip with her cello to play music? The only one I know tough enough to tackle such an unlikely challenge when many her age believed rocking in a chair was an adventure was my mother. No one could match her determination and drive. When she set her mind to it, no task was outside her reach. Those that had the pleasure and joy of knowing her know that she was one of the toughest women on earth. She was a quiet, diminutive, soft-spoken, "Katie-bar-the-door", alpha-female. She never quit. She never gave up. She may have suffered a setback from time-to-time, but it only increased her determination.

She suffered a setback on February 14th. She died. I have no doubt she'll regroup and pursue new challenges for a long time to come. This time, however, she'll reach new heights through her three sons and her many friends who look to her memory for strength and inspiration in their lives. As we go through life, we meet a select few people with an indomitable spirit that through their example help guide us through difficult and challenging times. My mother was one of those rare individuals.

Jean "Elizabeth" Schenk was the third of four daughters born to William Clarence and Tella Jane Radcliffe. When she arrived on July 25, 1924, the family had recently moved to Detroit, Michigan from Cleveland, Tennessee where work was hard to find in the aftermath of World War I. It was in Detroit she went to grade school and high school. It was there also that she met her first and only true love, her cello. Her older sisters played other instruments. Her father had played clarinet with John Philip Sousa's famous military band. Her mother was the pianist and vocalist in the family band. They needed a cello to fill in the bottom and her courtship with music began. One of her proudest memories was of playing with the renowned Detroit Symphony Orchestra. She played her cello until well into her eighties when her fingers became too weak to manage the strings. The world's most famous cellist, Yo Yo Ma had smiled when he instructed me to make certain I stopped by my mother's house regularly to tune her cello after it had become difficult for her. And of course I did it lest I incur the wrath of both my mother and her "sweetheart", Yo Yo Ma. A picture of my mother in the arms of Yo Yo Ma hung by her door until the day she died.

She was truly one of the toughest women I've ever known. She hadn't a hint of "quit" in her character. On three occasions, I have been called to her bedside by doctors who told me, "There is little hope for survival." Once in the mid-1970's, I received a late night phone call from a doctor at a hospital in Detroit. My mother had been hit head-on by a drunken motorcyclist doing approximately 100 mile per hour. "It is unlikely she'll survive until morning," he said. I quickly dressed and drove from East Lansing to Detroit. Somehow, the tenacious lady miraculously pulled through.

On another occasion, she began to experience an organ failure as a result of an incurable disease she'd unknowingly contracted from the blood transfusions given in the previous incident. She apsed into a coma and laid unresponsive for seven days in the Mayo Clinic Hospital in Phoenix, Arizona. My brother and I got the word late on Thanksgiving Day 2006. Brian immediately caught a flight from Detroit and I left San Diego for Phoenix. We met at the airport and drove together to Mayo. For seven days, we sat vigil as hope of my mother's survival diminished. The doctors said that if there was any significant chance of recovery, her coma would end in three days or less. By the seventh day, we knew hope was gone. I was to meet with the doctors on the morning of the eighth day to discuss letting her finally die. That evening, Brian went alone to my mother's room and said his painful, tearful and final goodbye to the woman who had brought him into the world. He then flew home to deal with another urgent matter in Michigan.

The next morning, Liz and I walked out the door for our last trip to the hospital. For some inexplicable reason, I picked up my mandolin, an instrument tuned just like a cello. I snuck it into the hospital room and quietly played music at my mother's bedside. I wistfully played some of her cello favorites for more than an hour before the team of doctors arrived for our meeting. I doubted my mother could hear, let alone process, the music, but something spurred me on. We met with the doctors and listened to their rather grim outline of the state of affairs. "There is no reasonable hope for her recovery," one said. "It's probably time to honor her wishes, remove her from all support systems and let her die peaceably."

I agreed, but said I'd like to call my brother and let him know before I gave them the go ahead. Liz and I went to lunch and I called Brian. He was in sad agreement and I returned to the hospital to give my consent. We rounded the corner and walked into her room. She was sitting upright, eyes wide open. She greeted us. "Hi! How are you?" she said. "Would you keep playing?" I played on until my fingers bled. She had again defied nature and done the impossible. She was super-human.

As the ravages of time waged war on all of us, she was given no quarter. In August, she fell and broke a hip. She underwent major surgery and those of us close by worried about her ability to defeat such adversity at eighty-six years of age. But again, like the tide, she came back. She worked, she struggled and she fought her way back. Although she kept her house in San Diego, she took an apartment in Scottsdale. One evening after a dinner at a local restaurant, she came home. When she started to fall backward, she instantly thought of avoiding injury to her tender hip. She landed on her other hip and broke it. The following day, she again underwent major surgery. The battle back from this setback proved to be too great even for this magnificent fighter. She died a month after her oldest and only remaining sister had died.

A couple of hours before she died, she asked for a taste of ice cream. She had her sense of humor right up to the end. She then laid back and asked me to play the mandolin again. This time she knew it was only for comfort. The last song I played for her was the first song she ever played for me on her cello – *Ashokan Farewell.* Some will know this as the theme music from the series on the Civil War, but to me it will always be *Mom's Song*.

For eighty-six years, she made it a habit of doing things that couldn't be done. She sailed her boat on the Great Lakes. She even defied gravity as she piloted her planes high above the clouds. She traveled the world. She met people easily and loved learning about them. She was a tom-boy, a lady, a tough guy, a soft embrace, a gentle song. In the years past when I used to travel the world climbing the big mountains, it was my mother that by her example had shown me that the summit was an attainable goal. It was her hand that led me up the icy walls. It was in her arms and with her proud gaze upon me that I arrived at the mountain top. From this time forward, whenever I look up toward the lofty peaks, I will see her standing there smiling. I will hear her beautiful music. I will feel her gentle touch.

She leaves three sons, seven grandchildren, four great-grandchildren, a cat and a long list of friends around the globe.

Appendix C

The following is an extended family tree of Jean Elizabeth Radcliffe.

Descendants of Andrew B. Ratcliff

Generation 1

1. ANDREW B.[1] RATCLIFF was born on 18 Sep 1848 in North Carolina. He died on 15 Feb 1926 in Tenga, Georgia. He married Mariah Bethier Phillips on 24 Mar 1867. She was born on 14 Jun 1846 in Tenga, Georgia. She died on 10 Mar 1918 in 8 Miles from Cleveland, Tennessee (Chilcutt?).

Notes for Andrew B. Ratcliff:
Farmer and a pastor of a Methodist church close to home. Licensed and ordained in October 1870 and preached until he retired.

The 1870 Census showed real estate valued at $100 and personal property valued at $100.

Buried at Moore's Chapel Methodist Church Cemetary in Tenga, GA.

Notes for Mariah Bethier Phillips:
According to a handwritten note from a family member around 1960, the Phillips were "black Irish", i.e., "Spanish in Ireland with black hair and blue eyes".

Andrew B. Ratcliff and Mariah Bethier Phillips had the following children:

2.   i.   JAMES HENRY[2] RATCLIFF was born on 18 Jan 1868 in Whitfield County, Georgia. He died on 28 Jan 1948 in Cleveland, Tennessee. He married Maranda Naomi Broomfield, daughter of William V. Broomfield and Sarah Louisa Sprinkle on 08 Sep 1889 in Cleveland, Tennessee. She was born on 10 Dec 1871 in Cleveland, Tennessee. She died on 26 Jul 1908.

3.   ii. JOHN RUFUS RATCLIFF was born in 1870 in Georgia. He married MARTHA JOHNSON.

4.   iii. CHARLES W. RATCLIFF was born on 12 Dec 1872 in Georgia. He died on 04 Jan 1948 in Cleveland, Bradley, Tennessee, USA. He married MARY JANE MAXWELL. She was born on 01 Feb 1873. She died on 15 Jul 1953.

     iv. JESSIE RATCLIFF was born in 1875 in Georgia. He died about 1880.

          Notes for Jessie Ratcliff:
          Died young

     v.   WILLIAM J. RATCLIFF was born on 19 Jun 1875 in Georgia. He died on 26 Aug 1898.

     vi. MARTHA RATCLIFF was born in 1879 in Tennessee.

     vii. THOMAS H. RATCLIFF was born in 1879.

     viii. LEVI RATCLIFF.

5.   ix. CAROLINA ELIZABETH RATCLIFF. She married (1) ROBERT PALMER in Youngstown, Ohio. She married VEST.

     x.   THEA DOCEA RATCLIFF. She died in 1963. She married E. L. Wallace in Marietta, Georgia.

Generation 2

2.   JAMES HENRY[2] RATCLIFF (Andrew B.[1]) was born on 18 Jan 1868 in Whitfield County, Georgia. He died on 28 Jan 1948 in Cleveland, Tennessee. He married Maranda Naomi Broomfield, daughter

of William V. Broomfield and Sarah Louisa Sprinkle on 08 Sep 1889 in Cleveland, Tennessee. She was born on 10 Dec 1871 in Cleveland, Tennessee. She died on 28 Jul 1908.

Notes for James Henry Ratcliff:
A jeweler for 60 years after serving a six year apprenticeship under W.O. Horner of Cleveland, TN. He then went into business for himself and sold the store in the fall of 1946. Three weeks after his retirement, he suffered a stroke and lived for another fifteen months.

According to my mother (Jean Elizabeth Radcliffe), when Maranda died, James Henry married her identical twin, Amanda. However, the 1910 census showed him married to "Louie M. Ratcliff" age 34 and living in Cleveland, TN. He apparently married her in 1908 or 1909.

James Henry Ratcliff and Maranda Naomi Broomfield had the following children:

6.   i.   WILLIAM CLARENCE[3] RADCLIFFE was born on 27 Jun 1897 in Cleveland, Tennessee. He died on 10 Oct 1967 in Ann Arbor, Washtenaw, Michigan, USA. He married Tella Jane Goodner, daughter of Gerome Lee Goodner and Adrienne (Ada) Mae Fullbright on 09 Mar 1918 in Cleveland, Tennessee. She was born on 22 Aug 1899 in Cleveland, Tennessee. She died on 15 Dec 1986 in Detroit, Michigan.

7.   ii.   CECILE LOUELLA RATCLIFF was born on 14 Dec 1903 in Cleveland, Tennessee. She married Vernon Shanklin on 05 Apr 1931 in Cleveland, Tennessee.

8.   iii.   LETHA VIOLA RATCLIFF was born on 21 Sep 1905 in Cleveland, Tennessee. She died on 08 Jul 1983 in Knoxville, Knox, Tennessee, USA. She married Walter C. Spicer on 25 Jun 1929.

3. JOHN RUFUS[2] RATCLIFF (Andrew B.[1]) was born in 1870 in Georgia. He married MARTHA JOHNSON.

John Rufus Ratcliff and Martha Johnson had the following children:

        i.   STELLA[3] RATCLIFF.

        ii.   LEOTA RATCLIFF. She married OTIS LINDSEY.

        iii.   SALLY RATCLIFF. She married BILL MORRIS.

9.   iv.   ANN RATCLIFF. She married THOMAS MCPHEETERS.

10.   v.   ELLA RATCLIFF. She married BURCHFIELD.

11.   vi.   EMORY RATCLIFF was born on 21 Apr 1894. He married NELL CLIMER. She was born on 21 Jun 1897.

        vii.   LLOYD RATCLIFF.

12.   viii.   N. T. RATCLIFF.

4. CHARLES W.[2] RATCLIFF (Andrew B.[1]) was born on 12 Dec 1872 in Georgia. He died on 04 Jan 1948 in Cleveland, Bradley, Tennessee, USA. He married MARY JANE MAXWELL. She was born on 01 Feb 1873. She died on 15 Jul 1953.

Charles W. Ratcliff and Mary Jane Maxwell had the following children:

        i.   IRA[3] RATCLIFF. She married ROY RIDEN.

        ii.   BESSIE RATCLIFF. She married ROGERS.

      iii.   ESSIE RATCLIFF. She married SMITH.

5.   CAROLINA ELIZABETH[2] RATCLIFF (Andrew B.[1]). She married (1) ROBERT PALMER in Youngstown, Ohio. She married VEST.

     Vest and Carolina Elizabeth Ratcliff had the following children:

      i.   WILLIAM[3] VEST.

      ii.   ALBERT VEST.

Generation 3

6.   WILLIAM CLARENCE[3] RADCLIFFE (James Henry[2] Ratcliff, Andrew B.[1] Ratcliff) was born on 27 Jun 1897 in Cleveland, Tennessee. He died on 10 Oct 1967 in Ann Arbor, Washtenaw, Michigan, USA. He married Tella Jane Goodner, daughter of Gerome Lee Goodner and Adrienne (Ada) Mae Fullbright on 09 Mar 1918 in Cleveland, Tennessee. She was born on 22 Aug 1899 in Cleveland, Tennessee. She died on 15 Dec 1986 in Detroit, Michigan.

     William Clarence Radcliffe and Tella Jane Goodner had the following children:

   13.   i.   VIRGINIA[4] RADCLIFFE was born on 23 Oct 1919 in Lynch, Harlan, Kentucky, USA. She died on 18 Jan 2011 in Greensboro, NC, USA. She married HARRY FISHER. She married LLOYD RANDLES.

         ii.   MARION AILEEN RADCLIFFE was born on 26 Mar 1922 in Dearborn, Wayne, Michigan, USA. She died in Sep 2007 in San Francisco, California, USA. She married LAWRENCE ROUBLE. He died in Jan 2000 in San Francisco, California, USA.

   14.   iii. JEAN ELIZABETH RADCLIFFE was born on 25 Jul 1924 in Detroit, Michigan. She died on 14 Feb 2011 in Scottsdale, Arizona. She married FRANCIS JOSEPH JONES. He was born on 06 Jan 1925 in Whitmore Lake, Michigan. He died on 03 Feb 2012 in Troy, Michigan. She married JOHN SCHENK.

   15.   iv. EVELYN JANE (PRISCILLA) RADCLIFFE was born on 16 Nov 1929 in Detroit, Michigan. She died on 02 Aug 1990 in Eugene, Oregon. She married WILLARD KENNETH SPLITTSTOESSER.

7.   CECILE LOUELLA[3] RATCLIFF (James Henry[2], Andrew B.[1]) was born on 14 Dec 1903 in Cleveland, Tennessee. She married Vernon Shanklin on 05 Apr 1931 in Cleveland, Tennessee.

     Vernon Shanklin and Cecile Louella Ratcliff had the following children:

      i.   ROBERT LEWIS[4] SHANKLIN was born on 17 Jan 1932. He died on 01 Mar 1933.

      ii.   RUTH LA VON SHANKLIN was born on 05 Apr 1934. She died on 12 Jul 1936.

      iii. VAUGHN DOUGLAS SHANKLIN was born on 24 May 1937.

8.   LETHA VIOLA[3] RATCLIFF (James Henry[2], Andrew B.[1]) was born on 21 Sep 1905 in Cleveland, Tennessee. She died on 08 Jul 1963 in Knoxville, Knox, Tennessee, USA. She married Walter C. Spicer on 25 Jun 1929.

     Walter C. Spicer and Letha Viola Ratcliff had the following children:

      i.   JIMMIE CHANDLER[4] SPICER was born on 22 Apr 1930 in Harlan, Kentucky, USA. He died on 19 Nov 1966.

      ii.   MARY ANN SPICER was born on 21 Apr 1933. She married MEL BUNTON. She married DON GORDON.

9. ANN[3] RATCLIFF (John Rufus[2], Andrew B.[1]). She married THOMAS MCPHEETERS.

   Thomas McPheeters and Ann Ratcliff had the following children:
   - i. JAMES[4] MCPHEETERS.
   - ii. THOMAS MCPHEETERS.
   - iii. IRENE MCPHEETERS.
   - iv. MILDRED "TOOTIES" MCPHEETERS. She married JOHN RAMSEY.
   - v. ROSE EUGENE MCPHEETERS.
   - vi. MARY LOUISE MCPHEETERS.
   - vii. RUTH MCPHEETERS.

10. ELLA[3] RATCLIFF (John Rufus[2], Andrew B.[1]). She married BURCHFIELD.

    Burchfield and Ella Ratcliff had the following child:
    16. i. RUTH[4] BURCHFIELD. She married HARRY KILKPATRICK.

11. EMORY[3] RATCLIFF (John Rufus[2], Andrew B.[1]) was born on 21 Apr 1894. He married NELL CLIMER. She was born on 21 Jun 1897.

    Emory Ratcliff and Nell Climer had the following children:
    - i. CECIL DELMER[4] RATCLIFF. He married AEDEL CARSON.
    - ii. RUBY IVELLA RATCLIFF. He married CLARENCE HARVEY.
    - iii. JOHN DWIGHT RATCLIFF.
    - iv. HAROLD EDWIN RATCLIFF. He married EULA RANDOLPH.
    - v. FREDERICK EUGENE RATCLIFF.
    - vi. WILLARD GILBERT RATCLIFF.
    - vii. HELENA BRACE RATCLIFF.
    - viii. GLENWOOD ODELL RATCLIFF.
    - ix. CHARLES AUGUST RATCLIFF.
    - x. EMMA JEAN RATCLIFF.

12. N. T.[3] RATCLIFF (John Rufus[2], Andrew B.[1]).

    N. T. Ratcliff had the following children:
    17. i. JOHN[4] RATCLIFF. He married HELEN HENRY.
    - ii. LLOYD THOMAS RATCLIFF.
    - iii. LOLA RATCLIFF.

iv.   VELMA RATCLIFF. He married SIMMONS.

v.   ANNA LEE RATCLIFF. She married ROY DAVIS.

Generation 4

13.   VIRGINIA⁴ RADCLIFFE (William Clarence³, James Henry² Ratcliff, Andrew B.¹ Ratcliff) was born on 23 Oct 1919 in Lynch, Harlan, Kentucky, USA. She died on 18 Jan 2011 in Greensboro, NC, USA. She married HARRY FISHER. She married LLOYD RANDLES.

Notes for Virginia Radcliffe:
Virginia's given name at birth was Geneva Lee Radcliffe

Harry Fisher and Virginia Radcliffe had the following children:
  i.   HARRY CLIFTON⁵ FISHER was born on 23 Jul 1941.

  ii.   WILLIAM GEORGE FISHER was born on 10 Aug 1943.

  iii.   ROBERT JAMES FISHER was born on 05 Dec 1945.

  iv.   DOUGLAS C. FISHER was born on 12 Dec 1946.

Lloyd Randles and Virginia Radcliffe had the following child:
  i.   ANN⁵ RANDLES was born on 27 May 1956.

14.   JEAN ELIZABETH⁴ RADCLIFFE (William Clarence³, James Henry² Ratcliff, Andrew B.¹ Ratcliff) was born on 25 Jul 1924 in Detroit, Michigan. She died on 14 Feb 2011 in Scottsdale, Arizona. She married FRANCIS JOSEPH JONES. He was born on 06 Jan 1925 in Whitmore Lake, Michigan. He died on 03 Feb 2012 in Troy, Michigan. She married JOHN SCHENK.

Francis Joseph Jones and Jean Elizabeth Radcliffe had the following children:
  i.   HOWARD ALTON⁵ JONES was born on 23 Apr 1947 in Detroit, Michigan. He married (1) LUCY LLEWELLYN BYARD on 19 Nov 1967 in Northville, Michigan. She was born on 31 Oct 1948. He married (2) LEONOR DE LA TORRE on 01 Apr 79 AD in Reno, Nevada. He married (3) ROBERTA LAROSE in 1980 in Tucson, Arizona. She was born on 20 Jun 1946 in Ganado, Arizona. She died in Mar 1986 in Gallup, New Mexico. He married (4) ELIZABETH ANN MCCARTY on 15 Sep 1984 in Show Low, Navajo, Arizona, USA. She was born on 30 Jan 1954 in Phoenix, Arizona.

  ii.   BRIAN CLAY JONES was born on 16 Feb 1952 in Detroit, Michigan.

  iii.   JEFF FRANCIS JONES was born on 19 Feb 1954 in Detroit, Michigan.

15.   EVELYN JANE (PRISCILLA)⁴ RADCLIFFE (William Clarence³, James Henry² Ratcliff, Andrew B.¹ Ratcliff) was born on 16 Nov 1929 in Detroit, Michigan. She died on 02 Aug 1990 in Eugene, Oregon. She married WILLARD KENNETH SPLITTSTOESSER.

Willard Kenneth Splittstoesser and Evelyn Jane (Priscilla) Radcliffe had the following children:
  i.   WILLARD KENNETH⁵ SPLITTSTOESSER was born on 12 Sep 1947.

  ii.   CLYDE LEWIS SPLITTSTOESSER was born on 19 Sep 1950.

  iii.   TELLA JANE SPLITTSTOESSER was born on 26 Feb 1952.

    iv.   LYNN D. SPLITTSTOESSER was born on 27 Sep 1954.

        Notes for Lynn D. Splittstoesser:
        According to Lynn herself, there is some question as to paternity.

16.   RUTH[4] BURCHFIELD (Ella[3] Ratcliff, John Rufus[2] Ratcliff, Andrew B.[1] Ratcliff, Burchfield). She married HARRY KILKPATRICK.

    Harry Kilkpatrick and Ruth Burchfield had the following child:
        i.   HELEN[5] KILKPATRICK. She married JAMES HENRY BURCH.

17.   JOHN[4] RATCLIFF (N. T.[3], John Rufus[2], Andrew B.[1]). He married HELEN HENRY.

    John Ratcliff and Helen Henry had the following children:
        i.   GARY[5] RATCLIFF.

        ii.   JEFF RATCLIFF.

Descendants of Cyrus Goodner

Generation 1

1. CYRUS[7] GOODNER was born on 06 Mar 1851 in Chilcutt, Tennessee. He died on 09 Dec 1932 in Chilcutt, Tennessee. He married (1) JANE K. BREWER, daughter of Jefferson Brewer and Martha Dever on 04 Jan 1872. She was born on 16 Jul 1847 in North Carolina. She died on 07 Jan 1916. He married BELL. She was born in 1876 in Tennessee.

Cyrus Goodner and Jane K. Brewer had the following child:

2. i. GEROME LEE[2] GOODNER was born on 09 Sep 1876 in Chilcutt, Tennessee. He died on 01 Nov 1959 in Cleveland, Tennessee. He married ADRIENNE (ADA) MAE FULLBRIGHT. She was born on 10 Jan 1874 in North Carolina. She died on 10 Nov 1955 in Cleveland, Tennessee.

Generation 2

2. GEROME LEE[2] GOODNER (Cyrus[1]) was born on 09 Sep 1876 in Chilcutt, Tennessee. He died on 01 Nov 1959 in Cleveland, Tennessee. He married ADRIENNE (ADA) MAE FULLBRIGHT. She was born on 10 Jan 1874 in North Carolina. She died on 10 Nov 1955 in Cleveland, Tennessee.

Gerome Lee Goodner and Adrienne (Ada) Mae Fullbright had the following children:

3. i. BUFFORD MILLER[3] GOODNER was born on 02 Feb 1897. He died on 23 Feb 1974 in Cleveland, Bradley, Tennessee, USA. He married Ruth Tallent on 17 Jun 1943.

4. ii. TELLA JANE GOODNER was born on 22 Aug 1899 in Cleveland, Tennessee. She died on 15 Dec 1986 in Detroit, Michigan. She married William Clarence Radcliffe, son of James Henry Ratcliff and Maranda Naomi Broomfield on 09 Mar 1918 in Cleveland, Tennessee. He was born on 27 Jun 1897 in Cleveland, Tennessee. He died on 10 Oct 1967 in Ann Arbor, Washtenaw, Michigan, USA.

    iii. MARGARET GOODNER was born on 10 Jan 1903 in Cleveland, Tennessee. She died in Mar 1981. She married William H. McFadden on 24 Nov 1927.

5. iv. RUBY IRATE GOODNER was born on 09 Apr 1906 in Cleveland, Tennessee. She married Francis Geren on 30 Dec 1925 in Cleveland, Tennessee.

6. v. GEROME LEE GOODNER was born on 14 Nov 1909 in Cleveland, Tennessee. He died on 13 Sep 1949 in Orange, Florida, USA. He married DRUCILLA HAWK.

7. vi. SARAH EVELYN GOODNER was born on 15 Feb 1912. She died on 17 May 1952. She married Karl Reber on 17 Aug 1935 in Detroit, Michigan.

Generation 3

3. BUFFORD MILLER[2] GOODNER (Gerome Lee[2], Cyrus[1]) was born on 02 Feb 1897. He died on 23 Feb 1974 in Cleveland, Bradley, Tennessee, USA. He married Ruth Tallent on 17 Jun 1943.

Bufford Miller Goodner and Ruth Tallent had the following children:

   i. IRENE[4] GOODNER was born on 27 Oct 1944.

   ii. QUINTIN JEROME GOODNER was born on 09 Apr 1947.

4. TELLA JANE[3] GOODNER (Gerome Lee[2], Cyrus[1]) was born on 22 Aug 1899 in Cleveland, Tennessee. She died on 15 Dec 1986 in Detroit, Michigan. She married William Clarence Radcliffe, son of James Henry Ratcliff and Maranda Naomi Broomfield on 09 Mar 1918 in Cleveland, Tennessee. He was born on 27 Jun 1897 in Cleveland, Tennessee. He died on 10 Oct 1967 in Ann Arbor, Washtenaw, Michigan, USA.

William Clarence Radcliffe and Tella Jane Goodner had the following children:

8. i. VIRGINIA[4] RADCLIFFE was born on 23 Oct 1919 in Lynch, Harlan, Kentucky, USA. She died on 18 Jan 2011 in Greensboro, NC, USA. She married HARRY FISHER. She married LLOYD RANDLES.

  ii. MARION AILEEN RADCLIFFE was born on 26 Mar 1922 in Dearborn, Wayne, Michigan, USA. She died in Sep 2007 in San Francisco, California, USA. She married LAWRENCE ROUBLE. He died in Jan 2000 in San Francisco, California, USA.

9. iii. JEAN ELIZABETH RADCLIFFE was born on 25 Jul 1924 in Detroit, Michigan. She died on 14 Feb 2011 in Scottsdale, Arizona. She married FRANCIS JOSEPH JONES. He was born on 06 Jan 1925 in Whitmore Lake, Michigan. He died on 03 Feb 2012 in Troy, Michigan. She married JOHN SCHENK.

10. iv. EVELYN JANE (PRISCILLA) RADCLIFFE was born on 16 Nov 1929 in Detroit, Michigan. She died on 02 Aug 1990 in Eugene, Oregon. She married WILLARD KENNETH SPLITTSTOESSER.

5. RUBY KATE[3] GOODNER (Gerome Lee[2], Cyrus[1]) was born on 06 Apr 1905 in Cleveland, Tennessee. She married Francis Geren on 30 Dec 1925 in Cleveland, Tennessee.

 Francis Geren and Ruby Kate Goodner had the following children:
11. i. HAROLD LUSK[4] GEREN was born on 25 Oct 1926. He married MONTREY FLUMMER.

  ii. KAY FRANCES GEREN was born on 30 Dec 1934.

6. GEROME LEE[3] GOODNER (Gerome Lee[2], Cyrus[1]) was born on 14 Nov 1909 in Cleveland, Tennessee. He died on 13 Sep 1949 in Orange, Florida, USA. He married DRUCILLA HAWK.

 Gerome Lee Goodner and Drucilla Hawk had the following children:
  i. CHARLOTTE[4] GOODNER was born on 14 Jan 1932.

  ii. JANET GOODNER was born on 06 Nov 1936.

7. SARAH EVELYN[3] GOODNER (Gerome Lee[2], Cyrus[1]) was born on 15 Feb 1912. She died on 17 May 1952. She married Karl Reber on 17 Aug 1935 in Detroit, Michigan.

 Notes for Karl Reber:
 As of July 2010, Gerald lives in Cleveland, Ohio. Phone: 440.238.6507

 Karl Reber and Sarah Evelyn Goodner had the following children:
  i. KARLEE KAREN[4] REBER was born on 08 Aug 1944 in Detroit, Michigan.

   Notes for Karlee Karen Reber:
   As of July 2010, Karlee lives in Orlando, Florida. Phone: 407.850.9590
   Address: 3191 Cashmere Dr., Orlando, FL 32827

  ii. GERALD LEE REBER was born on 31 Aug 1939 in Wyandotte, Wayne, Michigan, USA.

Generation 4

8. VIRGINIA[4] RADCLIFFE (Tella Jane[3] Goodner, Gerome Lee[2] Goodner, Cyrus[1] Goodner) was born on 23 Oct 1919 in Lynch, Harlan, Kentucky, USA. She died on 18 Jan 2011 in Greensboro, NC, USA. She married HARRY FISHER. She married LLOYD RANDLES.

Notes for Virginia Radcliffe:
Virginia's given name at birth was Geneva Lee Radcliffe

Harry Fisher and Virginia Radcliffe had the following children:
    i.   HARRY CLIFTON⁵ FISHER was born on 23 Jul 1941.

    ii.   WILLIAM GEORGE FISHER was born on 10 Aug 1943.

    iii. ROBERT JAMES FISHER was born on 05 Dec 1945.

    iv.   DOUGLAS C. FISHER was born on 12 Dec 1946.

Lloyd Randles and Virginia Radcliffe had the following child:
    i.   ANN⁵ RANDLES was born on 27 May 1956.

9. JEAN ELIZABETH⁴ RADCLIFFE (Tella Jane³ Goodner, Gerome Lee² Goodner, Cyrus¹ Goodner) was
    born on 25 Jul 1924 in Detroit, Michigan. She died on 14 Feb 2011 in Scottsdale, Arizona. She
    married FRANCIS JOSEPH JONES. He was born on 06 Jan 1925 in Whitmore Lake, Michigan. He
    died on 03 Feb 2012 in Troy, Michigan. She married JOHN SCHENK.

    Francis Joseph Jones and Jean Elizabeth Radcliffe had the following children:
        i.   HOWARD ALTON⁵ JONES was born on 23 Apr 1947 in Detroit, Michigan. He married
              (1) LUCY LLEWELLYN BYARD on 19 Nov 1967 in Northville, Michigan. She was born
              on 31 Oct 1948. He married (2) LEONOR DE LA TORRE on 01 Apr 79 AD in Reno,
              Nevada. He married (3) ROBERTA LAROSE in 1980 in Tucson, Arizona. She was born
              on 20 Jun 1946 in Ganado, Arizona. She died in Mar 1986 in Gallup, New Mexico.
              He married (4) ELIZABETH ANN MCCARTY on 15 Sep 1984 in Show Low, Navajo,
              Arizona, USA. She was born on 30 Jan 1954 in Phoenix, Arizona.

        ii.   BRIAN CLAY JONES was born on 16 Feb 1952 in Detroit, Michigan.

        iii. JEFF FRANCIS JONES was born on 19 Feb 1954 in Detroit, Michigan.

10. EVELYN JANE (PRISCILLA)⁴ RADCLIFFE (Tella Jane³ Goodner, Gerome Lee² Goodner, Cyrus¹
    Goodner) was born on 16 Nov 1926 in Detroit, Michigan. She died on 02 Aug 1990 in Eugene,
    Oregon. She married WILLARD KENNETH SPLITTSTOESSER.

    Willard Kenneth Splittstoesser and Evelyn Jane (Priscilla) Radcliffe had the following children:
        i.   WILLARD KENNETH⁵ SPLITTSTOESSER was born on 12 Sep 1947.

        ii.   CLYDE LEWIS SPLITTSTOESSER was born on 19 Sep 1950.

        iii. TELLA JANE SPLITTSTOESSER was born on 26 Feb 1952.

        iv.   LYNN D. SPLITTSTOESSER was born on 27 Sep 1954.

              Notes for Lynn D. Splittstoesser:
              According to Lynn herself, there is some question as to paternity.

11. HAROLD LUSK⁴ GEREN (Ruby Kate³ Goodner, Gerome Lee² Goodner, Cyrus¹ Goodner) was born
    on 25 Oct 1926. He married MONTREY FLUMMER.

    Harold Lusk Geren and Montrey Flummer had the following children:
        i.   HAROLD LUSK⁵ GEREN was born on 09 Jun 1947 in Cleveland, Tennessee.

ii.   TANNA GEREN was born on 03 Apr 1952. She married HUGHES.